MAJOR UNITED METHODIST BELIEFS

Revised Edition

Mack B. Stokes

ABINGDON PRESS
Nashville

MAJOR UNITED METHODIST BELIEFS: REVISED AND ENLARGED

This book is printed on recycled, acid-free paper.

STOKES, MACK B.
   Major United Methodist beliefs : revised and enlarged / Mack B. Stokes.
   ISBN 0-687-08212-9 (alk. paper)
   1. United Methodist Church (U.S.)—Doctrines. 2. Methodist Church—
United States—Doctrines. I. Title.
   BX8332.S685—1989
   230'.76—dc20
                                                              89-27294
                                                                   CIP

03 04 05 — 33 32 31 30 29 28

MANUFACTURED IN THE UNITED STATES OF AMERICA

Preface

We believe in revealed religion, experienced religion, and social religion.

Revealed religion is based on the Bible as God's living Word for our response. God has spoken, and we are called to hear and respond.

Experienced religion is personal religion. It is far more than forms, ceremonies, and second-hand religion. It means we trust in God to pardon us now because Christ died for us. It means the New Birth: the life transformed by grace through faith. It means the inner assurance that we are God's children now and are on our way to heaven.

Social religion binds us together with our fellow-Christians in public worship, Bible study, and praying for one another. It means reaching out to others by telling what Christ has done for us and by deeds of love and mercy. It means, by the indwelling of the Holy Spirit, "inward holiness" that leads to "outward holiness."

It is my prayer that this book, in its new edition, will continue to give understanding and inspiration to people in our local churches. It is my prayer also that it will open the way to a deeper appreciation of our Wesleyan heritage through which we may hear again God's call to "reform the nation" and to "spread scriptural holiness over the land." Above all, my earnest prayer is that those who read it and study it will feel anew the presence of God and join one another in bearing witness to our Savior's redeeming grace.

MACK B. STOKES
Atlanta, Georgia

TO

All My Students

Contents

Introduction

SINCE THIS BOOK first came out in 1956, many changes have taken place. The most important of these was the coming together in organic union in 1968 of the former Methodist Church and the former Evangelical United Brethren Church. This significant event inaugurated the present United Methodist Church.

I. A COMMON HERITAGE: HISTORY AND ORGANIZATION

This union was significant for many reasons. It brought together people who shared profoundly in their heritage, beliefs, and practices. It drew into a dynamic fellowship various denominational groups whose kinship with one another had become obscured with the passage of time. For example, back of The Evangelical United Brethren Church were two evangelical communities of faith—the Church of the United Brethren in Christ and the Evangelical Church.

Philip William Otterbein, Martin Boehm, and Christian Newcomer were among the great leaders in the United Brethren tradition. Jacob Albright was the towering figure in the Evangelical Association. There were internal differences along the way within each of the two churches, but these differences were transcended; and, in 1946, after years of study, prayer, and discussion, the two communions came together to form The Evangelical United Brethren Church.

The union in 1968 of that body with The Methodist Church was significant also because The Methodist Church was created out of the merger in 1939 of three separate communities of faith—the Methodist Episcopal Church; the Methodist Episcopal Church, South; and the Methodist Protestant Church. So the formation of The United Methodist Church brought together far more than the two churches that joined hands in 1968.

8

Over a period of many years scholars and church leaders on all sides experienced a growing awareness of the essential kinship in heritage, belief, organization, and practice of the churches involved. They were reminded of the close association of Francis Asbury and Philip William Otterbein, which led Asbury to request Otterbein to be among those who participated in his consecration as bishop. Otterbein agreed and was one of the four who joined in laying their hands on Asbury's head.

This kinship was so marked that during the formative years Asbury's group was sometimes referred to as "English Methodists" and the Otterbein-Boehm-Albright groups as "German Methodists." They all shared in the common concerns of the evangelical revival of vital religion in America. They preached the same gospel. They shared in emphasizing a personal, conscious, experiential relationship with God. Together they bore the brunt of ridicule and abuse because they condemned wickedness and called people to righteous living.

These churches were kin to one another also in their forms of government. The book of *Discipline* of Asbury's group was translated into German and served as a guide for the books of discipline of the various communions that finally came together to form The United Methodist Church.

II. A COMMON HERITAGE: BELIEFS AND PRACTICES

In response to my request for his observations, Professor J. Bruce Behney, former vice-president of United Theological Seminary, wrote two pages of thoughtful comments on the doctrinal kinship of the churches that came together to form The United Methodist Church. In one important paragraph he said:

> In spite of the fact that Otterbein and Asbury were very cordial friends, it seems that Otterbein was somewhat reluctant to follow closely the Methodist emphasis on the Twenty-five Articles, yet the content of their preaching was very similar. On the other hand, the former Evangelical Church took over the Articles and, with only relatively minor modification, accepted them also in close agreement.

Whether or not the Articles of Religion are viewed as central—and often they have been ignored in the heritage of the former Methodist Church—the theology was the same.

What basic beliefs did we share? What emphases did we have in common? I suggest, out of others that might be mentioned, six areas of agreement in doctrine and emphasis that are now brought to focus in The United Methodist Church.

1. The Bible as the Primary Basis for Belief

We share in holding that "Scripture is the primary source and criterion for Christian doctrine" (*The Book of Discipline of The United Methodist Church, 1996;* cf. Article V in *The Articles of Religion* and Article IV in the *Confession of Faith*). We share also in our way of approaching the Bible.

John Wesley gave his followers certain guidelines for interpreting Scripture in the *Forty-four Sermons* and in his *Notes on the New Testament.* These served at least as the negative limits of teaching and preaching. These *Sermons* and *Notes* were evangelical and Arminian. They emphasized religion as a conscious relationship with God through Jesus Christ, involving personal decision or response and the call to share these realities with others. They were also pragmatic, persuading people toward right living and ethical responsibility. From all sides the United Methodists have brought together these same biblical emphases. The Bible, then, is regarded as the primary source and norm of Christian belief. The Bible is to be understood, not with the mentality of a ferocious literalism, but with an eye to seeing it as God's living Word. It is to be interpreted in the light of tradition and Christian experience with the aid of reason. When we affirm that Scripture is the primary basis for belief, we mean to emphasize also what is at the heart of the biblical revelation: namely, the purpose of God coming to fulfillment in Jesus Christ. This is at the head of the hierarchy of biblical affirmations. This mystery is illuminated, not by tradition as a dead past, but by tradition as a developing understanding of Jesus Christ as Lord. The mystery of God's love in Christ is illuminated and brought home to each of us personally in Christian experience that is made available through the community of faith.

In view of some problems in the contemporary situation, it is important to add a word about reason as a basis for belief. We United Methodists hold that in many areas of human knowledge the rightful basis for belief is reason, broadly understood. For example, common sense enables us to know the world around us. On this level of practical reason we come to some understanding of the world of nature, the weather, civilization, traffic regulations, farming, other people, family life, earning a living, and so forth. Similarly, through the physical and behavioral sciences, we come to a more detailed and precise knowledge of things, events, and people. We believe also that Christians, like those who seek truth, can and should think about their idea of God. They can improve their understanding of God. They can discover solid reasons for believing in God. That is, by reason they may develop a theistic world view and show the intellectual weaknesses in the competing alternatives. We share in affirming a basic confidence in our God-given reason in these intellectual dimensions.

The twentieth century has been too much infected by the diseases of subjectivism and irrationalism. The words *existentialism, phenomenology, logical positivism, the analysis of language, death of God,* and so forth—though cumbersome and not easy to define—suggest how far we have succumbed to these maladies. To be sure, each of these terms suggests important contributions to our thinking in the modern world. But they are also infected with an incurable subjectivism and irrationalism. They illustrate our contemporary refusal to have confidence in the human mind's ability to attain some real understanding of God in relation to the universe and human beings. One practical consequence of this subjectivism and irrationalism is the resort to violence of deed and tongue so often manifested throughout the world. The tragedy here is that people act on the basis of emotion or ideology or private impressions rather than on the basis of reason and the will of God.

In this context, then, we United Methodists offer a twofold approach. First, within the community of faith the Bible, reasonably interpreted in the light of tradition and Christian experience, is the primary basis and guide. Second, we affirm confidence in reason as normative in the general quest for truth. This confidence in reason is felt even in regard to the formation of an overall world view with God as the ultimate Mind. This world view, attainable by the reasoning mind, lends support from outside, as it were, to what is already affirmed in the Bible. It enables us to communicate with those multitudes who are unavoidably involved in doubts and who are not yet receptive to the biblical revelation.

Reason never functions as a principle of salvation. Nor is it the final basis for belief within the community of faith. It is not a substitute for Scripture. Nor can it take the place of Scripture as the primal norm for Christian affirmation and conduct. But it has an immensely important role. Therefore the philosophical theologian and the thoughtful Christian are free to seek the truth about God, nature, and human beings that is open to rational discovery.

2. The Continuing Emphasis on Christian Experience

We share also in the continuing emphasis on personal salvation. Religion that is not experienced is not vital religion. The essence of Christianity is the experienced person-to-person relationship with God through Jesus Christ in the community of faith. From that profound inner reality flow the fruits of faith. Its vocabulary consists of the historic words: *repentance, faith, justification, regeneration, new birth, conversion, new creation, sanctification, holiness, growth in grace, responsible living in community, the life everlasting,* and any contemporary words that reach for the same experiential meanings. I am reminded again and again of Paul Tillich's remark that up to now the efforts to substitute new words for old ones in the Christian vocabulary have largely ended up by losing something of the depth of the original meanings. But here we must be open. For we have our eyes not on the words but on the experienced realities.

3. Christian Habits and Disciplines

Again, we share in the belief about practical Christianity that we cannot make much progress in it without Christian habits and disciplines. The unorganized life is ineffective. The undisciplined life is no more worth living than is the unexamined life. More will be said on this in Chapter 9.

4. From Inner Dynamic to Community Responsibility

We share further in the belief that the inner life necessarily produces outer results in keeping with it. The good tree, said Jesus, by its very nature produces good fruit. The bad tree necessarily produces bad fruit. We cannot make a good world out of bad people. Nor can we make a superior society out of mediocre persons. Structures may be changed—and ought to be, whenever indicated—but unless people are changed, little is accomplished. For any social structures, however well designed, are easily corrupted by evil persons or made cumbersome and inhuman by mediocre people.

So we United Methodists continue to urge on the contemporary world the need for the kinds of inner transformation, growth, and insight that, with the power of the Holy Spirit, necessarily issue in the responsible management of life, both personally and socially. As Wesley put it, the formula is: "inward holiness which leads to outward Holiness."

5. Arminian in Our Relationships With God

We share in a theology that is pervaded throughout by an essentially Arminian approach. "Universal redemption" (Christ died for all), "free grace," the ability to say yes or no to God and even to fall away from grace—these are the themes of Arminianism as against predestinarianism. This is not to say that the writings of Jacobus Arminius (1559–1609) actually shaped the minds of Wesley, Otterbein, Albright, and the others. It is rather to suggest that in his anti-predestinarian and free-grace stance Arminius represented a focal point in the controversy over this issue.

The measure of Wesley's appreciation of Arminius as a "great man," a sound thinker, and as the most important individual around whom the issue came to focus, is clearly visible in his creation and ardent promotion of the *Arminian Magazine.* He brought out the first issue in January, 1778, and continued it under his personal direction until his death in 1791. It was announced and carried forward as a magazine "consisting of extracts and original treatises on 'universal redemption.'"

Wesley felt that there were thousands of people halting between one opinion and the other, and he wanted to identify himself openly and sensibly on the Arminian side. When it was suggested that the title would turn many away, he pointed to the Roman Catholics and to many others on the Protestant side, both on the Continent and in England, who would welcome it. It was not until 1798, seven years after Wesley died, that the title was changed to the *Methodist Magazine.*

There is no doubt that those who joined hands to form The Evangelical United Brethren Church shared in this theology. Though they were very much influenced by Lutheran and Reformed traditions, they still showed their Arminianism in their emphasis on freedom, personal choice, and responsibility before God and one another. Paul H. Eller says that The Evangelical United Brethren Church was characterized by "a faith vitally related to the evangelical work of Luther and Calvin, modified by Arminianism and enriched by the Christian religious experience given common people." (*These Evangelical United Brethren,* Otterbein Press, 1950, pages 120–21.)

What we are dealing with here, of course, is the relationship between God and us in the process of salvation. What does God do and what do we do in this process? That is the question. Some have said that God does it all; we do nothing. This is selective election. At the other extreme are those who so minimize the divine action as to suggest that we must save ourselves. Everything is done by us and for us. So theology is reduced to anthropology, and instead of salvation by grace we are left to recover ourselves by our own decisions. That is, the aims and activity of God are translated wholly into our human aims and deeds.

We United Methodists turn away from both of these extremes and emphasize the one mighty theme that *God and human beings are interacting at every stage of life and grace.* Here is where the emphasis on the Holy Spirit comes in. The Holy Spirit is God present and at work on all levels of our lives. Even before we are Christians, the Holy Spirit is present along with the dynamics of human personality. John Wesley spoke of this as prevenient grace—the grace that goes before grace. Then, in the processes involved in becoming a Christian—including the awareness of guilt and inadequacy in repentance and faith—the Holy Spirit and the human spirit are mysteriously interacting. Similarly, though on higher levels, in the movement toward sanctification and Christian growth the Holy Spirit and the dynamics of human personality interact in the interest of creative advances in Christian living.

A word of caution is needed here. We United Methodists share with Christians of all eras in affirming the doctrine of justification by grace through faith. That is, we do not believe that we are forgiven for our sin by our own deeds but by the forgiving grace of God in Christ that is ours by faith. Our action and response, though indispensable in the process leading to justification or forgiveness, do not function as the principle of forgiveness, nor do they have merit in this process. Nothing we do can make God forgiving. It is God's nature, as revealed in Christ, to forgive. What we do is necessary to place us in a position to receive this divine blessing.

The basic point here is that God has chosen us to participate in creative advances through this present life. God's aim is, in evangelical and Wesleyan language, to promote scriptural holiness throughout the world. In other words, God summons us to participate in the realization of moral and spiritual values in community under Jesus Christ. So we are involved in lifelong adventures in Christian growth and in creative Christian service.

Throughout this entire process, then, the Holy Spirit and the human spirit are in mysterious yet experienced interaction. No one lives apart from the energizing, at one level or another, of the Holy Spirit. Christians live in increasing awareness of the presence of the Holy Spirit assisting them to move forward under Christ in the church and in the world. So we United Methodists join in affirming a total program of Christian living that gives continuing dignity for human beings and continuing glory to God.

6. The Call to Share What We Have Experienced

Once more, we United Methodists share in the desire to tell others what God has done for us. This apostolic commission has been a part of our heritage on all sides from the start. No one can read of Otterbein, Boehm, Albright, Wesley, and Asbury without being moved by their passion to evangelize, to share with others. Sometimes these men and their followers shared in small groups, sometimes in the open air, sometimes in barns or in large camp meetings and other gatherings, and sometimes in person-to-person witness. But always there was the sense of being summoned by God to evangelize, to tell the story of God's love as experienced in their lives.

Therefore on the contemporary scene we can hear again the call of God for United Methodists to be true to their heritage. For we, together with all Christian groups, have something of utmost importance to share with the world. We are called to communicate the message of salvation and responsible living.

That message includes at least three emphases. First, it includes the sharing of a total world view (including the basic belief in God as the only ultimate Being) without which human existence can have no enduring meaning. Second, it includes sharing Jesus Christ, the only one to whom we can commit ourselves without reservation and the only one through whom we mysteriously find our way from sin and mediocrity toward the highest experiences of God's grace. Third, the message we are called to share includes the promise and presence of the Holy Spirit to assist us in creative living and in using the only strategy for dealing with our human problems, namely, love informed by wisdom.

This message, this good news, the world desperately needs in these times. Therefore, we are called of God, who revealed it, to share it with courage, patience, resourcefulness, and passion. We are not to be discouraged in this great mission. For God is with us.

III. SOME REMARKS ABOUT THIS BOOK

These are the things in which we share. They form a kind of magnificent vision of the Christian religion that is urgently needed in these times of doubt, bewilderment, anxiety, disillusionment, and passivity.

The aim of the chapters that follow is to state in plain language what we believe and why we believe it. They are addressed to the general reader in The United Methodist Church—whether young, in middle life, or advanced in years—and to all other interested Christians with whom the thoughts here expressed will have much in common.

There is a note of urgency in what is said because both the gospel and the times require it. The book is written in the conviction that Christianity, in dynamic balance, offers the most magnificent option to men and women, young people and older people, who are looking with hope toward the twenty-first century. It is aimed to appeal, in a special way, to all who want to join that vast procession of people who are responding to the divine summons to rise above the paltry dimensions of mediocrity and to participate with God in doing a great work. For all of us are called to share in a magnificent destiny, both here and in the world to come.

On the doctrinal standards that we share as United Methodists, see *The Book of Discipline* (1996), Paragraph 62, Section 3, pages 57–72. For an excellent statement on our theological task, which reflects our interest in serious continuing theological reflection, see *The Book of Discipline* (1996), Paragraph 63, Section 4, pages 72–83.

CHAPTER 1

United Methodism's Enduring Significance

NOTHING IS EASIER to miss than an appreciation of what is always near. The air we breathe is ever present, so we seldom stop to think about it. We have come to take many liberties for granted, hence we rarely feel their true worth. So it is with our United Methodist heritage. We are so close to it that we frequently miss its glory and its abiding significance. "And sweets grown common lose their dear delight."

Additionally, broad-mindedness, which is rightly so dear to us, often leads us to feel that Methodism has nothing special to offer.

United Methodism as an organization is relatively new. It goes back only to John Wesley (1703–91), Philip William Otterbein (1726–1813), Francis Asbury (1745–1816), Jacob Albright (1759–1808), and their contemporaries. Why, then, speak of its abiding significance? Because it is a mighty force within the Christian fellowship.

There are no exclusively United Methodist doctrines. For, though we have distinctive emphases, we have no affirmations that are not also believed by other Christian groups. So some people ask, What is the place of United Methodism if it has no message all its own?

The answer to this is clear. While United Methodism repudiates any narrow sectarianism, it brings to the community of believers its own special gifts. What are these? Two key words tell the story: *vitality* and *balance*. United Methodism is Christianity with a vital balance. This is its abiding contribution to the Christian world.

But how did it come to stress this vital balance? Primarily because of the leadership of Wesley and of those who followed in his line of evangelical Christianity. Consider Wesley for a moment. He combined the warm heart with the consecrated mind. He was no roughhewn piece of lumber tumbling down the currents of history. He was a polished shaft. In this respect he followed in the line of Moses, the best-trained leader of the Old Testament, and of Paul, the best-trained mind in the New Testament.

John Wesley knew well that Christianity is always in danger of becoming either lifeless or one-sided. So the Methodism that he founded was one of the most earnest efforts to preach and teach a Christianity that is vital and balanced. Philip William Otterbein, scholar, master of Hebrew and Greek, shared in the spirit of Wesley in all this.

I. UNITED METHODISM IS VITAL CHRISTIANITY

United Methodism is vital because it calls us back to the one mighty fact of our religion: the grace of God in the hearts of people. It asks us to return to the glory of first-century Christianity so that we may sit at the feet of the apostles and learn from them the true meaning of our religion. Whenever United Methodism remains true to its genius, it persuades the world to enter into that same kind of vital religion. This is the altar round which the church is built. All else must be seen as a means of promoting apostolic Christianity in the world today. Christian doctrines, the Bible, public worship, the sacraments, and the programs of the church all exist to bring people into a living fellowship with God, to assist them to grow in grace, and to enable them to do a great work for God.

1. Vital Christianity: More Than Sound Doctrine

Some say that we should look for genuine Christianity wherever there is sound doctrine. According to them right belief is the most basic fact. So they tell us that we United Methodists, with our talk about the vital experience of grace, have drifted away from the true position of the church through the ages.

We believe in the importance of sound doctrine. We know that without great beliefs our souls shrivel up and die. We know also that the stream of life runs deeper than doctrines. The river of God flows far deeper than our beliefs. Vital religion is not in itself a matter of what we believe but of whom we trust. "Even the demons believe—and shudder" (James 2:19). Christian experience presupposes basic beliefs and goes beyond them.

2. Vital Christianity: More Than Belief in the Bible

Others say that we find genuine Christianity in accepting the truths of the Bible literally. They tell us that we United Methodists put this vital experience of grace, with its outreach in Christian conduct, above the Bible.

We believe in and exalt the Bible as the Book of books. But we insist also that a person may know the Bible from Genesis to Revelation and believe every sentence in it and still be far from the Kingdom. For we are not saved by the Bible but by the Savior of whom it speaks.

For example, why do we have the four Gospels? Because we cannot stand today in the presence of the historical Jesus in just the same way that the first Christians did. So we read about him in Matthew, Mark, Luke, and John. To be sure, the four Gospels contain other things besides materials about what Jesus said and did. They contain interpretation and the proclamation of God's good news. They do such a good job of picturing and recovering the historical Jesus that we too may remember him as the disciples did. These four Gospels exist to help us feel what the apostles felt when they walked along the roads with Jesus. (See John 20:31.)

In one way or another the whole Bible exists primarily to introduce us to the Savior.

3. Vital Christianity: More Than the Means of Grace

Again, there are some who find genuine Christianity in the unfailing power of the sacraments of baptism and Holy Communion or in the services and ministers of the church. Some stress baptism. Others stress the Lord's Supper. Our Roman Catholic friends see the heart of Christianity in the Mass where God's eternal work on the cross is each time mysteriously reenacted. Still others say that true Christianity exists in the services of public worship, where all join together in prayer and praise and inspiration. We United Methodists are told that in putting all our confidence directly in the Savior and in the assurance that is ours by the witness of the Spirit, we are missing something.

We United Methodists join other Christians in emphasizing the two sacraments, the worship services of the church, and the habits of prayer and meditation. We are convinced that everything ought to be done "decently and in order" (1 Corinthians 14:40). But we are forced to say that apostolic Christianity does not consist in ceremonies and forms.

Not even ministers and priests—for all their nearness to the Bible and to the sacraments—can in any literal sense give or withhold God's boundless grace in Jesus Christ. For ministers and laypersons, priests and confessors, are equally distant from the grace of God. They are equally near as well. Our assurance and growth in grace come from the Spirit in and through the community of prayer and faith.

4. Vital Christianity: More Than Good Works

Still others would find vital Christianity in moral precepts and good works. They tell us United Methodism misses the heart of the matter when it stresses the grace of God rather than good works.

We believe in the Christian moral life. We have not been activistic by chance. Our activism is the fruit of vital religion and is therefore not to be confused with it. United Methodism is vital Christianity because in it the strivings of the moral life and the wonderworking power of the Holy Spirit come together into a dynamic unity. Duty by itself is a small trickle. Morality by itself is a lazy brook. But the struggling stream of goodness within us can become a mighty river of God by the outpouring of the Holy Spirit in each of us.

II. UNITED METHODISM IS BALANCED CHRISTIANITY

When it comes to religion, people are always in danger of losing their balance. Our United Methodist forebears knew this. They preached and taught a kind of Christianity that, without losing its vitality, held its balance.

1. Balanced View of the Bible

We see this balanced Christianity first of all in our approach to the Bible. With all Christians we unite in affirming the great doctrines of Scripture. We recognize differences of interpretation on many points. We also commend four principles to aid us as we read.

First, the Bible is to be understood as the church's book. It has its being and meaning in and for the community of prayer and faith. The church has authorized it, preserved it, used it. The church, through centuries of prayerful study and reflection, has understood its central meaning as the revelation of God's redemptive love coming to fulfillment in Jesus Christ. In a balanced way, then, we United Methodists place ourselves as interpreters of the Bible in the main lines of Christian tradition.

Second, the Bible is to be understood not merely on the basis of a single verse or a few selected passages. Instead, we must rest our beliefs on the total insight of the biblical revelation. This total insight, as the church has understood it, includes as a central feature the revelation of the purpose of God for humankind in creation, redemption, and consummation. God is revealed in nature—that realm of reality known to us through sense—experience. In a unique way, God is revealed through the Bible—the realm of the spiritual world of prayer, worship, and grace.

Third, the Bible is to be understood as revelation for response. We may study it as literature or as history or in reference to scientific accuracy. From the standpoint of the deeper moral and spiritual meaning of the Bible, however, these miss the mark. For the point is that the Bible is God's living Word. A word is for communication. This living Word is communication from God calling for our response. The Word becomes effective when we begin to ask as we read, "What is God trying to say to me today through this passage?" or "What is God summoning me to do?" For the Bible is revelation for response to God.

A fourth principle that gives balance to our United Methodist belief is this: The Bible is to be understood as confirmed in Christian experience. The Bible is, in large measure, the witness of people over many centuries to what God has done. Its promises, its great passages, its insights, its practical teachings—all these are at last comprehended in their deeper meaning in the ongoing lives of believers. This keeps the Bible from being just another book and makes it the dynamic Word. It addresses itself to us now and in our particular circumstances today.

There is a marvelous balance in the habit of exalting the whole Bible, with Christ at the center of it, as the authority for our preaching, teaching, and living. At the same time it is a sure mark of sound thinking to read this book, as John Wesley and our forebears did, informed by the illuminating tradition of historic Christianity. It is also a mark of practical intelligence to understand the Bible in relation to our human situation today and to our growing Christian experience. For experience checks us in our errors. It shatters our illusions. It protects us against fanaticism. It is the one teacher to whom all of us go every day.

What Moses, the prophets, Jesus, and the apostles did and talked about becomes real in our contemporary experience. This helps us to share with them so as to gain a vitally balanced understanding of the Bible.

2. Balanced View of Conversion and Education

Again, this balance of United Methodism is seen in our emphasis on both conversion and education. In life itself these two are mingled together. However, there is always the peril of losing one or the other. Some people make the new birth everything. If we are not hurled suddenly into the Kingdom, they imagine that we cannot get there at all. They stress enthusiasm, feeling, and crucial decision. But they neglect the gradual processes of learning what it means to be a Christian.

This is one-sided, but it holds a profound truth in which we steadfastly believe. *The new birth has a momentous place in life.* When we see ourselves as we really are, we see the need of making an absolute commitment of our whole being to Christ. We need to be born of the Spirit.

On the other hand, our deep concern for education is seen in the vast amounts of talent and money we put into the literature of our Sunday school programs. We United Methodists deplore the present-day ignorance of the Bible. We are determined to give people throughout the world every chance to know that great Book. This is education.

This profound interest in an educated people is seen in the many colleges and universities that were founded and are operating under the support and inspiration of The United Methodist Church. We have determined not to allow our people to lose the vision of God in the midst of their studies in institutions of higher learning. We seek increasingly effective ways of communicating God's living Word in the contemporary world. We desire to influence the thinking of people at all stages and on all levels of education.

3. Balanced View of Personal and Social Christianity

This balance is seen further in the United Methodist concern for both personal salvation and social responsibility.

Individuals alone can be redeemed. God knocks on the doors of solitary souls. But the saved souls must do their duty while they live on this earth. As Jesus said, "We must work the works of him who sent me while it is day" (John 9:4).

Whatever harms people strikes at Christ and stirs the Christian into action. So United Methodism is concerned about war, broken homes, race prejudice, political corruption, organized crime, sexual promiscuity, poverty, pollution, the problems posed by overpopulation, alcoholism, drug addiction, and all forms of inhumanity.

4. Balanced View of Denominational and Ecumenical Efforts

We United Methodists believe in the ecumenical church. We are proud of our church. We are ashamed, however, of our failure to do our best to bring all the denominations into a closer unity of fellowship and action—"so there will be one flock, one shepherd" (John 10:16).

We rejoice in all forces that work to bring Christians together. For we know that we need the helping hands of one another to fight the battles of this present age. On large affirmations we shall agree. On small ones we shall agree to differ. On all practical matters we shall work together with others. Only then can we begin to say, "The kingdom of the world has become the kingdom of our Lord/and of his Messiah" (Revelation 11:15).

5. Balanced Doctrines

This balance is nowhere more in evidence than in our view of the great Christian doctrines.

We share with others the basic affirmations of the biblical revelation. We believe in Jesus Christ as Lord and Redeemer. We believe in the Holy Spirit as the power and presence of God ever working in us to lift us into higher dimensions of living. We believe that human beings are both created in the image of God and sinners and that, with God's help, they must choose whom they will serve and how they will live. We believe in justification by faith. We believe in the new birth. We believe in sanctification or holiness, not as a fixed state but as a dynamic movement by the power of the Spirit toward the realization of God's aims in us. We believe in the church as the people of Christ, the community of prayer and faith, wherein the Christian life is called into being, nurtured, and shared. We believe in responsible living in the world to the end that society may be transformed for the glory of God and the benefit of people. We believe in the life everlasting as a person-to-person adventure with God that begins here and now and that continues as a creative adventure with God and with those who participate with God in the kingdom of heaven beyond death.

In our own way we strive for a fully balanced understanding of these great Christian affirmations.

John Wesley and those who built on the foundations he laid did their work well. Wesley was a theologian, a reformer, a saint. His greatest ability, perhaps, was seen in his organizing genius. His most precious gift, however, was the vitally balanced Christianity that he preached and lived. Let us now take a closer look at the beliefs of United Methodists.

CHAPTER 2

We Believe in the Bible

THE TREE OF PROTESTANTISM roots in the Bible. In that soil alone does it flourish. Every time we try to plant it somewhere else, it withers away and dies. The Bible is the mainstay of our pulpits, the content of our Sunday school lessons, and the foundation of our devotional life. When we neglect it, vital Christianity suffers. When we exalt it, vital Christianity thrives.

We United Methodists join all Christian groups in viewing the Bible as the primary source and norm for Christian belief and conduct. We do not turn to the Bible because it will improve our cultural background, though it will do that. We read it prayerfully because we want to know God's will and purpose for our lives. In life we soon discover that our human treasures, like our fashions, come and go. Many books tumble off our presses and flow downstream into the vast ocean of oblivion. We are fascinated for fleeting moments by the literature of the day. However, in the midst of what comes and passes away, we find some things that are neither new nor old but ageless because they come from God. So the Bible abides.

> The grass withers, the flower fades;
> but the word of our God will stand forever (Isaiah 40:8).

I. THE BIBLE: AGELESS FOR ITS STORIES AND EVENTS

We United Methodists know, first of all, that the Bible is ageless because of the great stories and events through which God spoke and still speaks.

There is the story of Abraham, who, like an ancient Christopher Columbus, set out by faith to discover a new spiritual continent. There are the stories of Jacob and his vision at Bethel and of Joseph and his brothers. There is the sad account of the children of Israel in bondage in Egypt.

There is the unforgettable career of Moses. We see the babe saved from slaughter by an astute mother and adopted by Pharaoh's daughter. We see the little prince with all the advantages of the palace. We behold the young man seeing the bondage of his people and striking down an Egyptian. We see the frightened Moses fleeing to Midian only to be confronted by God while tending Jethro's flocks. Then we see Moses, the man of God, the greatest figure in the Old Testament, leading his people out of Egypt and governing them in the wilderness. We see the lawgiver, under the pressure of community life and under the inspiration of Almighty God, coming down from Mount Sinai with the immortal Ten Commandments. Then at last we read the sad story of Moses' wistful glimpse of Canaan and of his death somewhere perhaps on Mount Nebo's lonely slopes, where his worn-out body lies unfound and unmarked.

We read with fascination the stories of Deborah, a prophetess, a judge, and a mother in Israel; and of Hannah, the mother of Samuel; and Ruth, a foreigner who loved the God of Israel.

We United Methodists, along with others, return to the ageless stories of the kings. There is Saul, with his happy beginning and sad ending, who shows in his life and death the bitter fruits of disobedience.

There is David, the purehearted shepherd boy, triumphant with a round smooth stone over Goliath, the giant. There is David the mighty king, the miserable sinner, and the brokenhearted man, singing the songs of repentance for every human being.

There are all the other kings who "did what was evil in the sight of the LORD" and who thus stand as constant reminders of how power corrupts and of how the mighty have fallen.

We look eagerly to the stories of the prophets. From Amos, the roughhewn prophet of justice, to Jeremiah, the sensitive prophet of the deeper spiritual things, we see God's power working through these human instruments. Life had its tragedies and its defeats. But there was always the glory of the remnant, of the hope that roots in God, and of the promised Messiah.

Of course, we United Methodists never get tired of reading the stories of Jesus. There is the story of the angels singing, of the shepherds listening, of the wise men seeking. There is the beautiful story of the baby Jesus born in a stable and laid in a manger, while shepherds, wise men, all, came in to pay him homage.

There is the story of the twelve-year-old boy who loved the Temple and who lingered there to ask and answer questions.

There are the records of Jesus the stern yet winsome teacher and the great physician. He taught the ignorant, healed the sick, blessed little children, befriended women, and preached good tidings to the poor. That was his mission. (See Luke 4:18-19.)

Then there is the story of how Jesus was finally betrayed, arrested, slapped in the face, spat upon, laughed at, given a mock trial, and crucified as a common criminal between two thieves. There is the heartrending scene of the bleeding, suffering Jesus praying, "Father, forgive them; for they do not know what they are doing" (Luke 23:34).

At the last there is the unutterable beauty of the empty tomb and the risen Christ, who broke the bonds of sin and destroyed the power of death.

Once more, there is the story of Pentecost and the empowerment of the apostles and others for world evangelization. There is the story of Saul confronted by the risen Lord and receiving the new principle of power through Christ.

II. THE BIBLE: AGELESS FOR ITS REVELATION OF GOD'S PURPOSE

We United Methodists know that the Bible is ageless because, through its great characters and events, God has revealed the purpose for which God made us.

We can discover many things for ourselves. We can get some insights into what God is all about through experience and reflection. Yet there is no source like the Bible for disclosing God's purpose in creating us. Science and technology are immensely important, but they do not tell us why we are here. Explorations on the moon and on other planets could be among our finest achievements, but they reveal nothing about the meaning and purpose of our strange lives on this beautiful little planet. Psychology and social studies are important, but they do not provide an understanding of ultimate meaning and purpose. Culture and civilization say something to us about life and its direction, but they lack clarity and depth.

We can ride all the highways of the world or travel its waterways or fly its air routes and never discover why we are here. The Bible, rightly understood, reveals the meaning and purpose of human life. It teaches that God created us for a purpose. It is not enough merely to affirm that God created us. We must go on to the biblical teaching that God did so for the realization of a supremely worthy end. In this way the dynamic movement of God in pursuit of God's aims becomes visible. Purpose is the key idea in relation to God's creative action.

The Bible not only teaches that God made us for a sublime purpose. It reveals what that purpose is, namely, to realize moral and spiritual values in community. The words *in community* are important. God worked in and through the people of Israel. God spoke through Moses and the prophets in the context of community. The covenant was with the people of Israel. Jesus introduced the note of personal salvation into religion. He loved and served people one by one. Yet he also taught about the kingdom of God, and he summoned people to enter the kingdom of heaven. (*Kingdom* is an important biblical concept, even though it is not in common use today. It means that God rules all of the cosmos, even where his rule is not acknowledged.) All this means that God wants to realize moral and spiritual values in our lives in the midst of our involvement with our fellow human beings. For this reason it is no accident that, by the power of the Holy Spirit, the church was born at that first Christian Pentecost. It was the community of faith, the people of Christ. This principle is illustrated further by the fact that God made us and placed us in a family setting with community relationships from the start. The whole of our existence in society, with its political, economic, educational, recreational, and cultural dimensions, illustrates God's concern for the realization of values in community.

The Bible teaches also that all these values come to their highest realization under the leadership of Jesus Christ. His love and goodness guide the way. All achievements, however great, lose their glory unless they are aimed toward the well-being of people with which Jesus was concerned. All ideal values, such as friendship, humor, goodness, beauty, truth, and worship, have a life-subserving purpose under God. Wherever Jesus Christ is Lord, this is the direction that all human efforts take; namely, to benefit human beings for the glory of God.

Therefore, the Bible, in revealing the purpose for which God made us, gives us the sense of direction we need. This book guides us through this present life and opens the door to the creative advances of the future in the life after death. For God has a tender care never to abandon the valuable creatures formed in God's own image and for whom Christ died.

III. THE BIBLE: AGELESS FOR ITS MIGHTY AFFIRMATIONS

We United Methodists know that the Bible is ageless for its mighty affirmations.

We live in an age of secularism. By secularism I mean the idea that even if God exists, this makes no difference. Many things that are secular are good; many are bad. But secularism is a tragedy of the contemporary era.

In contrast to secularism and unbelief stand the mighty affirmations of the Bible. What are these great beliefs all about? First, the Bible tells us what we need to know about God. In a wonderful way it affirms God. It speaks of God as the Creator of the universe. God alone is Lord of all. Beside these tremendous affirmations of the Bible secularism is reduced to triviality.

Second, the Bible tells us what we need to know about ourselves. It insists that we never understand ourselves until we see ourselves in the light of God. Why? Because in the pure light of God three facts become clear. The first fact is that we are creatures. We are ever dependent on God. The second fact is that we are a very special kind of creature. We were made in the image of God (Genesis 1:26). This means that God made us for high and noble things and, above all, for himself. The third fact is that we are also sinners. The Bible teaches us that we have within us gravitational pulls away from God and from our own best ideals. We have passions and strivings that are at war with God's plan for us. The Bible tells us that in the midst of these inner conflicts and strivings we have the power of choosing which road we will take, whether to go where God is going or to go our own way. We are sinners because we take the wrong road. We are made to conquer evil, with God's help, but evil conquers us. From beginning to end, the Bible holds us to our responsibility for turning away from God.

Once more, the Bible tells us what we need to know about the meeting of God and us. For the vast redemptive powers of God are freely offered to everyone in Jesus Christ.

The Bible is a book about God. It is a book about us. It is a book about the meeting of God and us. It will never let us forget that God has made us for himself.

We United Methodists glory in the biblical affirmation that *God has taken the initiative in our behalf.* There is no greater thought than this: Long before we thought of God, God thought of us. We find this truth beautifully expressed in that simple little verse, "We love because he first loved us" (1 John 4:19).

What is most beautiful of all, God's redeeming love is free to all who repent and hold fast to the Savior. This is why we speak of the grace of God. God's love is freely given to all who trust God. The Bible declares the glory of God and tells us of God's wonderwork in Jesus Christ. It offers deliverance to everyone, not by the power of any human being, but by the grace of God in Jesus Christ. "For God so loved the world that he gave his only Son, so that everyone who believes in him may not perish but may have eternal life" (John 3:16).

IV. THE BIBLE: AGELESS FOR ITS MINISTRY TO HUMAN NEEDS

We United Methodists know that the Bible is ageless because through it God meets us where our needs go deepest.

For every moral and spiritual need of the human heart there is an answering passage in the Bible. Just as the world in its many-colored beauty can satisfy every human longing for beauty, so it is with the Bible and our hunger for spiritual truth. It meets us in our many moods. It goes with us wherever our temptations take us. It confronts us in our sin. In the lonely hours of the night the exalted beauty of its passages sings us to sleep.

When grief comes our way, we take up that Book and hear the voice of God. When we walk through the valley of the shadow of death, which is sometimes worse than death itself, we read and know that we are not alone.

When heavy responsibilities are placed upon us, we turn to the Bible and find the strength we need. When there is the call to do a great work for God and we totter on the brink of cowardice, we take up that book and read and know what must be done. When the burdens of suffering human beings press in on us, we read of the One who denied himself. Then we return to our tasks rejoicing that we can share in the work of God.

Those who have longed for chastity have turned to the story of Joseph. Those who have wanted patience have learned from Job. Political leaders who have felt their love of power threaten their characters have looked at Moses and learned how to be kingly in authority and humble in spirit. Those whose consciences have been dead have read Hosea and Amos and felt their moral strength restored. Those who have lost their courage have seen the face of Stephen and have become soldiers of the cross again. Those who have become weak in well-doing have retraced the long hard journeys of Paul and have heard him sing, "I was not disobedient to the heavenly vision" (Acts 26:19). Those who have hungered and have thirsted for forgiveness and eternal life have knelt at the foot of the cross and looked into their Redeemer's face.

V. CONCLUDING OBSERVATION

Against this background, we believe in the immense importance of the sacred Book. The Bible has not only guided the church but also given a special quality to our Western culture. The very idea of having this Book as the basis of our belief and practice means that we look beyond nature, beyond civilization, and beyond ourselves to God for our ultimate hope and destiny. The presence of the Bible in the church and in the nations communicates something of our desire to live in the world under God. We may not live up to it, but it is at least the declared basis of our belief and conduct.

CHAPTER 3

We Believe in God

UNITED METHODISTS JOIN all Christians and the people of all high religions in believing in God. We believe that the one true God is the Ground and Lord of this universe. Back of the starry heavens above, under the earth beneath, in and through the energies of the whole universe, and in our life within there is the living God.

I. WHY WE BELIEVE IN GOD

We believe in God because of our heritage in the Bible. We United Methodists also believe in God because it makes sense to do so.

We are not at all impressed with atheism. Why? Because it has never made a single positive contribution to the world. It is a doctrine of denial rather than affirmation. Besides that, it does not make sense. In contrast to it, we say two things. First, we believe in God because the Bible and the Christian home have taught us to believe. Also we believe because our best thinking demands it and our experience confirms it.

Some say, "God is too great to be known by us." We declare that God is too great not to allow us to know at least something of God. We know that there is mystery. We are sure that there are many things about God that we shall never know. But we hold that God has made himself known to everyone who takes a good look at the world. (See Romans 1:19-20.)

Others say, "You should not give arguments for God because that makes the arguments greater than God." That sounds very pious, but we cannot accept it. Why not? Because nobody is making the arguments greater than God. The arguments have to do not with God but with our belief in God. We United

Methodists insist that to those who have doubts we need to show that our best thinking leads us toward belief in God.

If there is good reason for believing in God, we ought to talk about it. If we are called foolish for believing, we ought to indicate the reasons for our belief. For in addition to our scriptural heritage, we United Methodists place confidence in our reason as a basis for belief.

Why do we believe in God? Basically for three reasons that are intertwined in mutual support.

1. It Is Intuitively Plausible

It is intuitively plausible to believe in God. We do not have to be philosophers to see this, though that may help. Here the basic idea is that we perceive by a kind of immediate insight that the finite requires the Infinite. Just as a leaf requires a tree, a blade of grass the earth, and a whitecap the ocean, so the finite requires the Infinite, the passing demands the Enduring, the imperfect calls for the Perfect.

Anselm (1033–1109), who is famous for presenting the so-called ontological argument for the belief in God, rendered an important service. He showed that there is an inherent difference between the idea of God and the idea of everything else. He brought to clarity what most people perceive intuitively; namely, that God cannot be thought of as not existing. If that were possible, God would not be God. Of everything else, we know that it might not have existed.

For example, a tree in a front yard now exists; but at one time it did not exist. In the future it will cease to exist. So it is with people. There is no inherent reason why we have to exist. If we live after death, this will be because God wills it and not because we must necessarily continue to be. In fact, of the entire universe we may say that it need not be. There is nothing about it that requires it to exist. God might have created numberless other universes. But God created this one. There may come a time when God's work with this one is finished; and it will cease to be. So this universe, though presently existing, does not necessarily have to be.

This is not the case with God, however. God has to be, else God could not be God. We perceive this intuitively. When we ask the question, Who made God? we show that we do not understand the meaning of the word *God.* For if God could be made by something else, then God would be less than God, surely a logical contradiction.

2. It Is Intrinsically Reasonable

Again, it is intrinsically reasonable to believe in God. That is, in the light of the total evidence and in the light of the major options, it makes sense to believe in God. Consider briefly some of the important kinds of evidence that point to theism (the belief in God).

First, there is the evidence from the physical universe and the creatures in it. This matter is very complicated, but let me be as plain as I can. In our common-sense experiences with the things around us, we come to realize that we are living in an ordered world. We seldom stop to ask why it is orderly or how it came to be so; but, when we think about it, we realize that this calls for explanation. That is, we want to understand how it is possible for there to be an ordered world. Scientists, as they explore the cosmos beyond the reaches of common sense, also presuppose and discover an orderly universe. They are not generally philosophers and theologians, so they might not ask why there should be an orderly universe.

Another way of putting it is this: What does the human mind require to explain an ordered universe when there are infinite possibilities for chaos? The best answer I know is that the creative activity of God alone is adequate to explain this. We may experiment with the only oft-repeated option (unless we abandon the search altogether), namely, that the universe is a product of chance or of impersonal processes. When we do, however, we realize that we have not discovered any adequate explanation. So we have to go with our best thinking and say that only God can explain this universe.

Out of many others, three further facts require explanation. The first is the fantastic fact that we can know the world around us. It is not in our minds, but we know it. The universe, from its tiniest particles to its largest galaxies, is intelligible. Einstein spoke of this when he said, "One may say the eternal mystery of the world is its comprehensibility." This is all so close to us that we are apt to miss it. We simply accept the fact that we know the world around us. We see trees, cars, other people, the stars, and let it go at that. How is it possible? By chance or impersonal process? Never. The best explanation I know is that God, the ultimate Mind, is at work in and through the universe to make it a continuing medium of communication. That same God created our minds and made them capable of receiving the messages from nature, so there is mind at both ends of the line. God explains what otherwise goes unexplained.

A second fact is that of creativity. A. N. Whitehead, whom some called the greatest philosophical mind of the twentieth century, said that he could not accept atheism because it did not explain the amazing creativity in the universe. How can new things emerge? The universe is characterized by creative energy, energy producing novelty. Can this be explained by chance or impersonal process. Of course not. Here again the dynamic energy of God, marked by purpose and intelligence, is the most reasonable explanation we have. Indeed, it makes more sense than any competing alternative.

A third fact (in addition to the basic fact of an ordered universe) has to do with values. Beauty and goodness are among the truly ideal values. They should be experienced by all. But why should this be a universe in which we experience beauty when there are infinite possibilities for ugliness and disharmony? Yet the physical world is so made that it can satisfy every longing for beauty in the human spirit. It also yields itself to our desires to create beauty. The painter has the materials. The builder can shape wood, brick, stone, steel, and aluminum into magnificent buildings. The musician can create instruments that bear ordered sounds. The writer has pen or typewriter and paper. Why all this coordination, both in nature and in us, toward the production of beauty? The ancient psalmist perceived the answer when he said,

> The heavens are telling the glory of God;
>   and the firmament proclaims his handiwork.
> Day to day pours forth [the story],
>   and night to night declares knowledge (Psalm 19:1-2; line 3
>   was suggested by *The Interpreter's Bible*, IV, page 102).

There is also goodness. This comes to focus in human beings. Why should we be moral creatures? Would this be possible if chance or impersonal energy were ultimate? Of course not. Yet here we are, moral beings. This is not to say that we actually live as we should. Everyone knows that we do not. What we have in mind is that we recognize the ideal of goodness, are capable of responding to it increasingly, and cannot be satisfied without coming to terms with it. This is not merely something that we have learned, an accident of our upbringing. Rather, like our intellect, it is a capacity with which we were born. It requires life situations to come to expression, but it is more than these.

As human beings, we ask moral questions. Is it right or wrong to lie, steal, cheat, kill, and so forth? Did we do the right thing? Where did we go wrong? What we mean here is that, in a way not possible for monkeys, dogs, horses, whales, and birds, we have a capacity for the moral life. But why should this be the case? Is it because of chance or impersonal processes? Never. Our minds perceive that something more is needed to explain this presence of the moral nature in us. That something more is God. When we realize that God is good, we perceive that as Creator, God is the ultimate Source of all goodness and moral aspiration. Again, it makes sense to believe in God.

3. It Is Experientially Confirmable

People have not only thought about God and talked about God; they have experienced God's presence and power. The best evidences here are the lives of the saints. These are those who are worthy of the imitation of all people. They are selected as the best evidences because in any line the best lives are authoritative. In science we do not look to dabblers but to the Pasteurs, the Marie Curies, the Einsteins, the best. So is it here. No witness to the reality of God would be complete without that of the saints and of all those who have followed in their line. For they tell us not only of the God of the universe. They speak also of the God of Abraham, Isaac, and Jacob; of Moses, David, and the prophets; of the apostles; and, supremely, of the God and Father of our Lord Jesus Christ.

From the start we are impressed with the number, quality, similarity, and contributions of those who have reported the continuing presence of God in their lives. They compose a vast multitude. Some are famous and some are not. All adorn the world with the beauty, goodness, and triumph of their lives—often under the most difficult circumstances.

The Bible is full of such examples. Job, the suffering saint, speaking out of the depths of his affliction, says, "I know that my Redeemer lives" (Job 19:25). The psalmist gives his simple witness, "The LORD is my shepherd" (Psalm 23:1). Many who have walked with God come and go. We call them prophets. Then Paul speaks. Everyone has been eager to hear him. His face is radiant. His speech is deliberate but forceful. He says, "We know that all things work together for good for those who love God" (Romans 8:28). He pauses for emphasis and continues, in effect, "I am sure, from long experience, that nothing—no matter how bad or tragic—can separate us from the love of God in Christ Jesus our Lord." (See Romans 8:38-39.) Millions have followed in his line.

II. SUMMARY

Because of these and similar considerations, it is no accident that there has been a long succession of first-rate minds in Western thought who have beheld the vision of God. There was Plato, the most gifted man ever to take up philosophy. There was Aristotle. There were all those philosophical and theological minds of the West who have joined some from the East in affirming a theistic world view. These thinkers, following in a magnificent line, cannot be lightly ignored by thoughtful people.

There were also the great minds of literature: Dante, Shakespeare, Milton, and others. There were scientists like Kepler, Newton, Pascal, and Pasteur; and there are many of the best men and women in our own day. Yes, and there were the great religious and saintly souls of the ages: Moses, Deborah, Ruth, Isaiah, Jeremiah, the psalmists, the apostles. There were Augustine, Thomas Aquinas, Luther, Calvin, and John Wesley. In our own time there was Mother Teresa. All of these join the vast company who have affirmed the reality and power of God. So we confront a long succession of witnesses telling the story of the greatness and glory of God. (See Hebrews 12:1.)

We are left to ponder these things in silence. When the truth sinks in, the impact is tremendous. For we begin to see that no comprehensive belief comes to the human mind with better credentials than the belief in God. Atheism does not stand up under careful thought. To think about it is to refute it. Agnosticism, which says, "We do not know," is intellectual timidity. Leave out the Creator, and we have to resort to the myth that all this order and ingenuity in the universe come "somehow" from unconscious processes. That is sheer credulity. Affirm the Creator, and the mind recognizes that it has the real explanation. While the fact of natural evil presents a problem for the person who believes in God, it is as nothing compared to the difficulties that stand in the way of anyone who tries to account for human beings and the universe without God.

Besides this, the cumulative witness of millions of religious people through the centuries is unanswerable. As we have seen, the clearest witness here comes from the saints, because these men and women have entered into the religious life—experimented, if you will—more persistently than the others. They are in a better position to know than anybody else. There is only one thing to do with the cumulative testimony of honorable people: accept it. We may sit in the armchair and doubt, but this much is sure: *We can neither establish nor destroy in the armchair what has been verified in the laboratory of the human soul.*

III. WHAT GOD IS LIKE

In what kind of God do we believe?

1. God: The Ultimate Personal Spirit

We believe that God is the Ultimate Spirit. God is ultimate because God is the beginning and the end, "the Alpha and the Omega" (Revelation 1:8). God alone is self-existent.

God is Spirit. Many people are so dazzled by what they see that they miss the glory of the unseen. But what do we mean by the word *spirit?* Here we get the best clue by looking at ourselves. We have bodies, but we are spirits. For example, all of us have a purpose for doing something. Yet while we can see what we do, we can never see our purpose. Why?

Because it is spiritual. So is it with our souls. They are unseen spirits.

Nature is that realm of reality that is accessible to us through the five senses. But there are realms of reality not known through sensual experience.

We see the physical world, but we cannot see God. So we believe in the unseen God who sustains us. "God is spirit, and those who worship him must worship in spirit and truth" (John 4:24).

2. God: The Ultimate Person

We United Methodists believe that God is the Ultimate Person.

From beginning to end the Bible teaches that God is a living person. God is the Creator, not merely the first principle of things. God is the Sustainer of the universe, not merely a cosmic process. God is love, not merely the moral order. God is the Ultimate Person, not merely a system of ideals or a cosmic process.

What do we mean by this? Of course we do not mean that God is limited as we are. We mean rather that even on our human level a person gives us the best clue that we have to what God is like. A person knows.

God, the Ultimate Person, knows the universe and identifies the children of God. If God did not know us, there could be no vital religion. God is our Father who knows each member of his family.

God loves God's children. The question is often asked, "Does God really care about our little lives on this earth? Isn't God too great for that?" The answer is that God is too great *not* to love us. The greater the gardener, the more he or she likes each particular flower in the garden. The greater the God, the more intimately God knows and loves every one of God's children.

When we say that God is a person, we mean also that God acts. God is not some far-off static deity serenely contemplating the tragedies of nature and history. God is dynamically present in all events and in every life. It is not enough to speak of God as a process. But, whatever else we may say of God, God is inherently dynamic. The God of the Bible is the God who acts.

God does things. God creates, sustains, provides. Besides huge projects throughout the universe, God acts daily on our lives.

God rebukes, forgives, redeems, strengthens, promises, confirms, delivers, keeps, judges, challenges. God breaks the bonds of death and summons us to a creative adventure with God in paradise. So God is carrying forward God's purposes. As Jesus said, "My Father is still working, and I also am working" (John 5:17).

3. God: The Ultimate Sovereign

We believe that God is the Ultimate Sovereign.

Whatever else the Bible tells us about God, it will not let us forget that God alone is the sovereign of the universe and the Lord of all the earth. God alone has the last word. God alone is God.

At the same time, we affirm the freedom and responsibility of people under God. Some tell us that if God is sovereign, God controls and determines in advance whatever we do. We United Methodists could never believe that God binds us hand and foot and allows no place for our responsible action. We are not puppets on the stage of life. We hold that God's sovereign command created us free beings with the power of saying yes and no. The truth is that it takes a greater God to make people free than to make them puppets. Our freedom, far from robbing God of power, is one of the surest signs of God's sovereignty.

God is the Ultimate Sovereign. In all matters God alone commands our complete devotion.

4. God: The Ultimate Love

God is not only supreme in power but also in love. God's power is an unfailing expression of love. This is the meaning of the revelation of God in Jesus Christ. The prophets before him caught fleeting glimpses of this. For example, Zechariah saw it when he spoke for God, saying, "Not by might, nor by power, but by my spirit, says the LORD of hosts" (Zechariah 4:6). God speaks through the Suffering Servant (Isaiah 53). God requires of us, in contrast to power and might, that we do justice, love kindness, and walk humbly with God (Micah 6:8). The full meaning of God as love was not available to us until Jesus Christ revealed it in his self-giving love that led him to suffer and die for us.

When we push forward toward the deeper meaning of all this,

we come to see that the love of God revealed in Jesus Christ is the same love that is back of the universe. Love created it in the first place. Love sustains it. Love carries it forward into the future. The love of God made known in Jesus Christ is ever present with us to forgive, to sustain, to empower, and to conquer death. God has spoken through Jesus Christ in the accents of a moral universe. Not all is clear to us on this because of the fact of pain, suffering, and natural evil. But deeper than these mysteries is the biblical affirmation that God is self-giving love. This divine love is the only final basis for hope, for openness to the future.

IV. GOD: THE HOLY TRINITY

We United Methodists believe in the Trinity. We believe also that there is a great difference between trinitarianism and unitarianism. What does all this mean?

Let us begin with the historic doctrine of the Trinity. God is three-in-one. Is not this a contradiction? No, but it is a mystery. There is only one God. But, on the basis of the Bible, Christians across many centuries have urged that we must say more than that. For the one true God is revealed in different ways in relation to our lives. So, in struggling to express this fact, Christians have recognized three interrelated but distinct kinds of activities in which God is engaged. What are they?

Before answering that question, we need to note that Christians have insisted that these three kinds of divine activities come out of differentiations within God. A person may be one individual. Yet he or she is complex. A person thinks, feels, decides. These activities are rooted in three distinguishable features of one being. This is an analogy only. It is merely suggestive. In some mysterious way God is three-in-one. God is one Being with at least three structural differentiations. Of course, if we could know everything about God, we might see that God's being is so rich as to have innumerable other differentiations. But God's infinite love and wisdom have revealed the three great characteristics of God's nature that bear most importantly on our human needs. What are those three characteristics?

They are God the Father, God the Son, and God the Holy Spirit. God as Father is Creator and Sustainer of the universe.

God the Father thus is revealed in the created universe and in a general concern for all creation and all humanity. God the Son is the redeemer and re-creator of our souls. God is revealed in Jesus Christ. This revelation is different from the revelation in the universe of God's general providence. God the Holy Spirit is God in our hearts and minds. Here God is present most clearly within the community of prayer and faith where Jesus Christ is Lord. God as Holy Spirit is specially related to the mission of the church. For there God works to bring home to us the glory of salvation in Jesus Christ. The Holy Spirit fills us with the longing to reach out and draw others to the new life in Christ. The Holy Spirit forms us into the worshiping and serving community for the glory of God.

We believe that it makes a great practical difference whether we are trinitarians or unitarians. Why? Because we need to know specifically what God expects of us and promises to do for us and through us. In unitarianism God's aims and actions are not sufficiently clear for a decisive response. In trinitarianism we know that God created us for a great purpose. We know that God has acted and still acts in our behalf through Jesus Christ to forgive us and to re-create our souls. We know that God is ever present to magnify Christ as Lord and to move us to tell of God's redeeming grace. We know the responses of faith and commitment that God expects us to make.

From this we can see that the doctrine of the trinity is pragmatic. It specifies the practical differences God makes when we open ourselves to God and put our trust in God. All this is essential to vital or experienced Christianity. In unitarian religion, revelation tends to be for contemplation. It seeks to satisfy the intellect. In trinitarian religion, the revelation of God, without sacrificing the interest in the intellect, leads to our total response and commitment to the divine summons.

CHAPTER 4

We Believe in Jesus Christ

WE UNITED METHODISTS believe that the greatest fact of history was the coming into the world of Jesus Christ. The most sublime events were those that began in a stable, continued on a cross, and ended with an empty tomb. The birth of a babe in a strange little village marks the great divide in time. All that went before was B.C.; all that followed, A.D.

We hold that in Jesus Christ eternity bared its secrets to us. In him all tyranny over our souls was given the sign of its defeat. In him everyone can claim the right to receive the grace of God and to become a new creation.

Some tell us that Jesus' earthly life was not very important. They say he wrote no books, composed no songs, drew no pictures, carved no statues, amassed no fortune, commanded no army, ruled no nation. Yet we know that Jesus spoke as no one else had spoken and that he lived and healed and died as no one else had done.

He who never wrote a line has been made the hero of unnumbered volumes. He who never drew a sketch has been the inspiration of some of the finest paintings put on canvas. He who never carved in stone has lived to be the architect of the world's most beautiful cathedrals. He who never wrote a song has put music into the hearts of nameless multitudes. He who never established an institution is the foundation of the religion that bears his name. He who refused the kingdoms of this world has become the Lord of millions. He who never wove a napkin has been woven into the civilizations of the world. Yes, he whose shameful death scarcely produced a ripple on the pool of history in his day has become a mighty current in the vast ocean of the centuries since he died.

He was so winsome that children loved him, so gentle that women were comforted by him, so stern that rough people took notice of him, so compassionate that the multitudes pressed on him, so courageous that the powers of entrenched evil trembled before him, so pure that sinners saw God in him, so faithful that he went up that lonely heartbreaking road to the cross, and so triumphant that twenty centuries after his life on earth his cross still stands as "sovereign emblem over all."

What is the significance of this Jesus? Was he merely a Jewish peasant who lived long ago, who captured the multitudes by his amazing powers of healing, and who astounded the people by his teachings? Was he just a man who combined with the force of a prophet the gentility of a saint?

We United Methodists join the ancient apostles and all other Christians in affirming that "in Christ God was reconciling the world to himself" (2 Corinthians 5:19). With the earliest Christians we too stand before Jesus, the Son of man and the Son of God.

How shall we say it in the language of our day? We know that no single formula can tell the full truth here. For all great truths require more than one approach to them. The church has never been fully satisfied with what it has said about the meaning of Jesus Christ as Lord and Redeemer. Without presuming to give an exclusive formula, we believe that one of the best insights here can be plainly stated. We believe that the eternal God was uniquely and redemptively present in what Jesus said and thought and did. God was in the birth and in the actual life that Jesus lived.

I. GOD IN THE COMPASSION OF JESUS

With this in mind, we notice first of all the compassion that Jesus had for the multitudes, and we see God there.

Who were these people that Jesus loved? They were not cultured folk. They were poor, sick, and enslaved by the tyranny of conventions. Jesus loved them. He suffered with them. He felt the pangs of their hunger, the privations of their poverty, the anguish of their diseases. He had compassion on the multitude. (See Matthew 15:32; Mark 8:2.)

How touchingly this is brought before us in a great scene just outside the city of Jericho! Bartimaeus, a blind beggar, the son of Timaeus, was sitting by the way on the outskirts of that ancient city. (See Mark 10:46-52.) During the quiet hours of many a day he had perhaps recounted in his thoughts the incidents told him about Jesus. How frequently had he longed to be near this Jesus! On that particular day, perhaps, he told himself to let his imagination linger no longer on the Galilean. For he would never come his way. Not long afterward, he heard the sound of an approaching crowd. What did it mean? The multitudes who were following Jesus were moving toward the spot where Bartimaeus sat. Amid the hustle and bustle of the passing throng this poor man asked anyone who would answer, "What's all the crowd about?"

The reply came back, "Oh, it's a man from Nazareth who is passing by. I think they call him Jesus."

Bartimaeus's voice caught in his throat, and for a moment he could not utter a sound. Then the words burst forth on the air like so much pent-up energy that was suddenly released: "Jesus, Son of David, have mercy on me!" Some, hearing him cry out to Jesus, shouted harshly at him, "Quiet, blind fool! Jesus has no time for the likes of you!"

The Gospel writer puts it wonderfully when he says, "But he cried out even more loudly, 'Son of David, have mercy on me!'" The ears of the Master, tuned long in advance to hear the cries of people, were pierced by the desperate sadness of the voice that uttered those words. He stopped and said, "Call him here." Bartimaeus cast away his garment, leaped to his feet, pushed through the throng, and, trembling, stood in the presence of Jesus. Everyone knows the rest of the story, how Jesus bade him go his way and how immediately there appeared before his wondering eyes a world of color, of forms and shapes and people. When John's disciples came to Jesus and asked, "Are you the one who is to come, or are we to wait for another?" Jesus' reply revealed again the measure of his compassion: "The blind receive their sight, the lame walk, the lepers are cleansed, the deaf hear, the dead are raised, and the poor have good news brought to them" (Matthew 11:3, 5).

Now was that compassion that Jesus had for the people merely the strange exaggerated mood of a Jewish peasant who lived two thousand years ago? No. That was the eternal God clothed in flesh and blood and showing us everlasting compassion. *That was God in Christ!*

II. GOD IN JESUS' ESTIMATE OF PEOPLE

Again, we United Methodists notice how Jesus estimated all people as belonging essentially on the same level before God. He was no respecter of persons. It mattered not whether they were rich or poor, strong or weak, young or old, men or women, one race or another, Jesus viewed them all as on the same level before God. So he struck mightily against that chronic plague of the human race that has led the proud people of all the ages to look down on their fellow human beings.

Jesus knew that some people were more gifted than others. The parable of the talents tells that story.

According to Jesus, the Pharisee had no vantage point before God that entitled him to despise his brother tax collector. The rich had no right to hold their special privileges over the poor. Not even Caesar was entitled to lordship over the souls of people. Men had no birthright that did not also belong to women. Adults walked no pathway into the kingdom of God that little children might not tread. The children of Abraham had no claim on the power of God that was not also available to the Canaanite woman or the hated Samaritan. The chief priests and elders had no seats in heaven that the harlots and the outcasts might not fill. Jesus saw all people as on the same level before God.

Here Jesus fought against one of the worst attitudes of people toward their fellows. The secular mind has never fully realized how much people owe to Jesus for what freedom they have.

Now was this estimate Jesus placed on all people merely the peculiar judgment of a Jewish peasant who lived centuries ago? No. We United Methodists believe that this was the eternal God showing in the Savior what God thinks of people. For "God shows no partiality, but in every nation anyone who fears him and does what is right is acceptable to him" (Acts 10:34-35). *This was God in Christ!*

III. GOD IN CHRIST'S POWER TO SAVE

There is an even deeper side of this. In Jesus Christ, God convinces people of sin, helps them to conquer sin, and draws them to himself.

We see this when we take a close look at the apostles. Jesus impressed them so much that after the Resurrection it seemed perfectly sensible to them to believe that the vast redemptive powers of Almighty God were now released to everybody through him.

Nothing seemed to make sense like the thought that the crucified and risen Lord was the promised Savior of the world. These disciples had heard Jesus speak. They had lived with him on the most intimate terms. Yet one of them could say to the multitudes, "God has made him both Lord and Messiah, this Jesus whom you crucified" (Acts 2:36).

In this we are impressed by the unrestrained confidence and boldness with which these apostles announced the gospel. They had known Jesus in the flesh. Yet it seemed to them perfectly proper to believe in him as the Savior of the world. No recorded fact could pay a higher tribute to Jesus Christ than that. No other fact could tell us more about the impact of Jesus on his disciples.

That was the eternal God redemptively at work in the Savior. No other language will tell the story. If we cannot fully understand it, that does not entitle us to the folly of denying it. We do not understand life, but we live it. Millions can witness to the forgiving, life-giving power of the Savior.

Is this mighty work of Christ merely the strange impact of a Jewish peasant out of the long ago? No. It is the eternal God at work redemptively in the living Savior. It is God in Christ forgiving and conquering sin and drawing us to himself. So Jesus said, "And I, when I am lifted up from the earth, will draw all people to myself" (John 12:32).

God is in Christ to pardon and transform sinners and to open new possibilities for everyone.

CHAPTER 5

We Believe in the Holy Spirit

WE UNITED METHODISTS share with all Christians in believing in the Holy Spirit. We believe that God is not only "high and lofty" (Isaiah 6:1) but also nearer than hands and feet and closer to us than breathing. At times we have neglected this doctrine of the Holy Spirit. When we have not neglected it, we have often misunderstood it. It would not be going too far to say that the doctrine of the Holy Spirit is the most neglected and most misunderstood vital doctrine of the Christian religion. Frequently we have not known what to say about the Spirit. But always we have been true to New Testament Christianity whenever we stressed the power and presence of the Holy Spirit. In order to see this clearly we must turn to the New Testament and retrace the steps of Jesus and his first disciples and Paul.

I. THE HOLY SPIRIT IN THE NEW TESTAMENT

The three primary sources of insight in the New Testament are these: (1) what Jesus taught, (2) what really happened at Pentecost, and (3) what Paul said. (See John 13–17; Acts 2:1-42; 1 Corinthians 12:1-3.)

We remember the times when Jesus promised the Holy Spirit to his disciples. He was facing the cross. He knew his earthly mission was to end soon, so he wanted to bind their hearts together in love and to strengthen them. We find the story in the Gospel of John. (See John 13–17.) Jesus promised them the comforting presence of the Holy Spirit. (See John 14:26.) They would never be left alone in the world. They would be supported and strengthened in all good things by the unseen Presence. As

Jesus said, "It is to your advantage that I go away, for if I do not go away, the Advocate will not come to you; but if I go, I will send him to you" (John 16:7). Here, of course, the word *Advocate* refers to the Holy Spirit. (The Greek word *Parakletos* is difficult to render into English.) Jesus also said, "When the Spirit of truth comes, he will guide you into all the truth" (John 16:13).

Jesus did not mean that the Holy Spirit would be like an encyclopedia, a vast source of information to us. Rather, he meant that the Holy Spirit would help us to know all we need to understand for our souls' salvation in Jesus Christ and for the basic direction of our lives on earth. Jesus went on to say, "He will glorify me, because he will take what is mine and declare it to you" (John 16:14; see also 14:26). Jesus made it impossible to separate the work of the Holy Spirit from his own person and mission. Jesus taught his followers that the Holy Spirit was sure to come and bring their minds and hearts to focus on Jesus himself and on the community that was to bear his name.

This promise was fulfilled on the day of Pentecost. Picture the scene. Jesus had been crucified. Judas had hanged himself. The eleven disciples and others had gathered in the upper room where they "were constantly devoting themselves to prayer" (Acts 1:14). Jesus had commanded them to remain in the city until they were "clothed with power from on high" (Luke 24:49). Fresh on their memory were the words of the risen Lord, "You will receive power when the Holy Spirit has come upon you" (Acts 1:8). Not long after that it happened: "All of them were filled with the Holy Spirit" (Acts 2:4). Peter, who tremblingly denied his Lord before a servant girl just a few weeks before, was now so transformed and empowered that he stood before the people of Jerusalem and delivered a powerful sermon. That same Jerusalem had rejected Jesus. Its religious leaders had brought about the crucifixion of Jesus. In such a setting Peter, with the others standing with him, spoke.

What really happened at that first Christian Pentecost? Some call attention to the sound from heaven "like the rush of a violent wind." Others think of the "tongues, as of fire" that appeared to rest on each one present. Still others think of how they "began to speak in other languages" (Acts 2:2-4). Clearly these were outer accompanying factors, not the inner reality. Whatever else the power of the Holy Spirit may be, it is beyond question an inner transforming force. So what we want to know is how those followers of Jesus were changed within.

We find the clue in what Peter preached when he stood before the multitude. He said, "Let the entire house of Israel know with certainty that God has made him both Lord and Messiah, this Jesus whom you crucified" (Acts 2:36). The real meaning of that Pentecost comes to light not merely in the first four verses of Acts 2 but in what began to manifest itself in the minds and hearts of Peter and the others. The Holy Spirit illuminated their minds so that, for the first time in any settled way, they grasped the fact that God had chosen to do a mighty redemptive work for the whole world through Jesus Christ. They had walked with him, sat at his feet, and broken bread with him. They had witnessed his resurrection and heard his promise of the Holy Spirit. The full meaning of the coming of Jesus Christ was not grasped, however. Then suddenly, they were made aware of the tremendous fact that he was the One through whom the whole world was to be redeemed. The power of God in their risen Lord was felt in their own hearts. The experience was overwhelming.

The Holy Spirit's unique mission of magnifying the Savior became an experienced reality in the hearts of those present. The followers of Jesus were formed into a community of prayer and faith based on this great good news. Three thousand souls were added to the fellowship that day (Acts 2:41). What happened, then, was that the Holy Spirit transformed their lives by illuminating them as to who Jesus really was and by enabling them to make a total commitment of themselves to the living Christ. In a true sense, that was the birthday of the church.

This is significant for United Methodists in a special way because of our emphasis on the experienced presence of the Holy Spirit. Outward signs and accompanying factors may be present, but the ageless glory of that occasion was the life-changing power of the new faith and total commitment to Jesus Christ wrought by the Holy Spirit. To be sure, those present played their parts too. They were there; they had a common memory of Jesus and talked together about it; they were receptive; and they responded. But the substantive power—without which that scene would have been nothing more than a gathering of bewildered people sharing their fears and disappointments—was the power of the Holy Spirit.

Paul, in his judicious and inspired way, perceived the inner meaning of that first Christian Pentecost when he said, "No one can say 'Jesus is Lord' except by the Holy Spirit" (1 Corinthians 12:3). The words *Jesus Christ is Lord* formed one of the earliest Christian confessions. Paul reminded the Christians at Corinth of what he had taught them; namely, that the primary mission of the Holy Spirit is to bring home to them the real meaning of that confession.

We United Methodists, then, believe that in Pentecost we confront a primal fact of Christian history. What people in their own strength alone could not do, they did under the power of the Holy Spirit. No wonder the earliest Christians talked so much about the Spirit. No wonder Paul asked, "Did you receive the Holy Spirit when you became believers?" (Acts 19:2). And no wonder centuries afterward another disciple could speak of that first Christian Pentecost as "an eternal moment in the destiny of mankind." For those disciples had entered into a new dimension of existence by the power of the Spirit. We too can feel the power of the Holy Spirit blowing new energies into our wills.

II. WHO IS THE HOLY SPIRIT?

What is the meaning of all this for us? What is the Holy Spirit? Rather, who is this Spirit?

The Spirit is God's nearness, made known and available in Jesus Christ. The Spirit is God close beside us, at work within us. We United Methodists believe that God meets us where we are and at every stage in our spiritual pilgrimage. The Holy Spirit is the unseen Presence rebuking us for every evil thought and deed, confirming us in every good thing, and summoning us to creative advances with God and our fellow human beings.

Another way of saying it is this: The Holy Spirit is the power of the risen Christ at work in our hearts. For we believe that this Spirit is far more than some vague force that stuns and shocks people. Paul set the pattern for our thinking here when he said that the Lord is the Spirit (2 Corinthians 3:18). He taught us to think of the Spirit as the living Christ at work within us. This saves Christianity from all those strange doings in the name of the Spirit that border on the magical and the hysterical. So the Holy Spirit is the mighty unseen power of the living God that makes for Christlikeness or holiness in our lives.

This basic biblical guideline is important because whenever Christians emphasize the inner spiritual life—as we United Methodists do—there are dangers of identifying the work of the Spirit with our own deep feelings and hunches. Almost every conceivable error of judgment or breakdown of intelligence has claimed to be the work of the Holy Spirit.

The Spirit guides us, but many times we do not really know how to distinguish between our own hunches or impressions and the authentic movement of the Spirit. The Spirit may heal our diseases, but we may deceive people into believing that we know the laws of his healing work. Speaking in tongues, or unintelligible sounds, may be manifestations of the Spirit when people are overwhelmed with the joy of the Spirit's presence. These activities are not at the heart of the New Testament teaching on the Holy Spirit, however. For the primary mission of the Holy Spirit is to magnify Jesus Christ as Lord in the community of faith and in the world. All else is secondary.

III. THE LANGUAGE OF THE HOLY SPIRIT

How does the Holy Spirit speak to us? What language does the Spirit use?

There are many languages in the world, and there are different languages that the Spirit of God uses in speaking to us. Yet many people never learn to hear them.

For example, there is the language of conscience. Some things are right. Some things are wrong. Some things that we stoop to are beneath contempt. Yet we try to justify ourselves in them. Anything to exalt our own beloved selves! Then the presence of the Holy Spirit, in the light of Christ, confronts us with ourselves as we really are. The Spirit is present also in our boredom, disillusionment, and despair. The Spirit meets us in our anxieties as well as in our hopes and dreams. This power of the Spirit, then, is at work to a degree in every human being. Even before the gift of God's grace there is this wonderful preparatory work of the Spirit. John Wesley called this work prevenient grace— which means the grace that is already present before we are really Christians. This is "the true light, which enlightens everyone" (John 1:9). It is the law of conscience that is written on the hearts of all (see Romans 2:15).

Thus God has not left us to ourselves. By nature, by birth, God has a claim on us and speaks to us in the language of conscience. God speaks in the language of beauty, of companionship, of culture and refinement, and of creative work in the busy affairs of daily life. Strange as it may seem, the Holy Spirit speaks to us even through sadness. The Spirit speaks in the plaintive language of loneliness calling us to fellowship. The Spirit whispers in the still, dark silence of our futility: "Children, the truth in Christ will make you free." During the long fearful hours when we walk through the shadow of death, the Holy Spirit speaks the language of comfort and peace. In the midst of our doubts the Spirit speaks the language of trust. In despair the Spirit speaks hope; in fear, confidence; in resentment, love.

The Holy Spirit works by various tugs and pulls on our souls in the course of daily living. The Christian has no more important responsibility than that of understanding the divine language that is spoken throughout each day.

Every impulse and motion of the Spirit is to draw us to God. The Spirit convinces us of the hopelessness of life lived without God. Why? To show us the truth of the new life in Jesus Christ. The Spirit shows us the awfulness of our sin—something we do not like to see. Why? To lead us from the darkness into the light of Christ. The Spirit strengthens every noble impulse in us by working quietly within our souls. Why? Because the Spirit's aim is to make the living Christ not merely a fleeting object of affection but the master impulse of our entire being.

The Holy Spirit empowers us through the church. The Spirit meets us in baptism when we are incorporated into the community of faith and in corporate worship, inspiring us through the words and music of the hymns. The Spirit leads us through the prayers spoken and unspoken, through the special music, through the Communion services, and through the sermons.

Few things are more important than learning how to understand the divine language. The Holy Spirit surely speaks to those who tune their ears to hear.

The Holy Spirit also speaks within our hearts the language of assurance. Paul put it this way: "When we cry, 'Abba! Father!' it is that very Spirit bearing witness with our spirit that we are children of God" (Romans 8:15-16). Hence, we know by the witness of the Spirit that we are children of God.

This is just what Wesley stressed. We United Methodists believe that we need not drift about on a sea of uncertainties. For we can know within ourselves that we belong to God and are in God's favor.

Wesley said something else here: "Let none ever presume to rest in any supposed testimony of the Spirit, which is separate from the fruit of it." So the Holy Spirit works in us to bear fruit.

IV. THE FRUIT OF THE SPIRIT

We believe that the Spirit of God daily works in our lives as what Augustine called "the good of all good." We rejoice daily in this fact. So the Spirit bears fruit through us. This is the nature of the Spirit.

What kind of fruit does the Spirit bear? Here Paul, who gave us our profoundest insights on the works of the Holy Spirit, must guide us. He said, "The fruit of the Spirit is love, joy, peace, patience, kindness, generosity, faithfulness, gentleness, and self-control. There is no law against such things" (Galatians 5:22-23; see also Romans 14:17). We may add to these the great Christian virtue of wisdom. For love implies wisdom.

We believe that these fruits are not, like apples and pears, gifts of nature. Nor do they come into their fullness out of our wisdom and culture. They go deeper than our moral life. The Spirit is present both in the refinements and duties of life. Our good manners and politeness are not enough, however, to do God's work in the world. The power of duty is merely a struggling stream compared to the tidal wave of God's grace that is needed. Around the turn of the twentieth century two men set out in the world to do a job for humanity. They were about the same age. One of them was Stefan Zweig of Austria. He drank from the cultural fountains of Europe. He knew the best that had been thought and said. After World War I, he dedicated himself to the fight against the "lunacy of war." He wrote books and became famous in many lands. Then along came Hitler and his armies to puncture the dreams of a Europe at peace. Those armies moved into Austria and Stefan Zweig moved out. He went to Brazil, where he hoped to build a new home. But on February 23, 1942, while contemplating Europe's spiritual plight, he committed suicide. He gave the world a kind of light, but his was a light that failed.

The other man was a missionary. Early in his life he felt the call to carry the ageless gospel to Korea. There he preached and taught and labored until, after some thirty years, he was instrumental in establishing nearly two hundred churches. Then war struck the Far East. Missionaries were brought home for reassignment. This man was called home and sent to a field in an entirely different part of the world. He had to learn a new language. Soon he was preaching there in the native tongue and carrying forward the work of God like a true soldier of the cross. He too gave light to the world, a light that did not lose its glow.

What was the difference? Phillips Brooks has given us a beautiful figure that tells the answer. One man was like a candle lighted from the finest altars of this world to produce an earthly flame. The other was like a candle lifted high up to the altar of heaven and there lighted with the divine flame.

The fruit of the Spirit comes not from ourselves alone but from the indwelling and unseen Presence. We United Methodists join all Christians who affirm this to be one of the most basic differences between vital religion and the secular perspective. We are commanded to love. Yet in ourselves we cannot fully do it. We are required to forgive. Yet in ourselves we cannot fully do it. We are required to forgive. Yet in ourselves we fail. We are called to serve. Alas, we fret over the miserable goals that end in self. Then comes the penetrating, pure work of the Holy Spirit to set us right and to give us the power of moving toward what we were made to be.

There is one more kind of fruit of the Spirit that, though implied, is not often openly stated. I have in mind the interaction between the Holy Spirit and the human spirit in the creative use of talents in every area of achievement. As we have seen, the primary and unique mission of the Holy Spirit is to magnify Jesus Christ as Lord so that scriptural holiness will be manifested through us. We must not allow anything to obscure that. For it is our mission to reform people by spreading scriptural holiness over the land.

Those who are brought into the newness of life through Christ have talents that are to be put to their best use. In view of the God-appointed human interest in art, literature, music, the performing arts, the sciences, politics, business, labor, recreation, and so forth, it follows that all human talents are to be used as creatively as possible for the glory of God and the benefit of people. The Holy Spirit assists us to make the best use of our talents and thus to claim them for the cause of humanity. It is no accident that among the highest flights of artistic, music, literary, intellectual, and cultural achievement have been those made under the influence of Christ.

Here again our built-in capacities are to be understood as quickened and guided by the divine assistance. This is the ultimate basis for an authentic Christian humanism.

The Holy Spirit, then, is the greatest force for righteousness and creativity in the world today. People everywhere desperately need this resource for creative achievement and service in these baffling times.

CHAPTER 6

We Believe in People

NOTHING IS EASIER than to lose faith in people. We United Methodists, however, join all Christians in holding fast to the God-given goodness that is in every human being.

We know that people are not good enough to be what they ought to be without God's help. We know also that the view of people as mean and sinful has its dangers. We are all sinners. Our sin becomes tragic only because we are much more than sinners. We have been created in God's image. In spite of our sin, that image is engraved on our souls by the act of Almighty God. By birth God has set a mark and seal on us and claimed us for himself. (See Genesis 1:27.)

I. ARE PEOPLE REALLY IMPORTANT?

It is not always easy to have a high opinion of people. Why not? Because our human estimates blind us to the full truth.

First of all, there are perspectives from which our human life seems like the merest trifle. For example, when we see ourselves over against the vast stretches of things in space, we are reduced to nothing.

Look at the stars, and we shrink to particles of dust. Our pride bursts like a pretty bubble. Before the heavens, where is the glory of the whole human race? Is it not rather a speck lost in space? This is not a new thought. The ancient psalmist said:

> When I look at your heavens, the work of your fingers,
>   the moon and the stars that you have established;
> what are human beings that you are mindful of them,
>   mortals that you care for them? (Psalm 8:3-4)

Again, we look backward into the past and forward into the future; and what we call our present is only a flickering candle in the wind.

Who knows how long God has been at work? Who can count the millions of people who were born, grew up, and died, and who are no longer remembered by anyone—unless God remembers them? Families, clans, and tribes have come and gone only to get lost in "death's dateless night." Nations have risen to power and glory only to go down. If we want to find the remains of most of the civilizations of history, we must dig them up from beneath the surface of the earth.

How short life is! How long time is! We are here today and gone tomorrow. Such a life as we have, like a speeding car, swiftly passes by. We are easily lost in the vast procession of the ages, and our days "are like a passing shadow" (Psalm 144:4).

Why all this talk about the dignity of human life? This too is not a new thought. For the ancient psalmist said,

> As for mortals, their days are like grass;
>   they flourish like a flower of the field;
> for the wind passes over it, and it is gone,
>   and its place knows it no more. (Psalm 103:15-16)

When we enter the moral world and see the depths of evil to which people can go, we question their dignity. Even on the simple levels of daily life there is a touchy pride in people that makes it hard to admire them. As so many people have pointed out, self-love is always with us. Writing about this self-love, La Rochefoucauld called it "one long and mighty agitation." For many, life is little more than the restless motions of selfishness.

Another common weakness is ingratitude. No matter how much is done for us, we are apt to be ungrateful. For we like to turn everything toward ourselves.

William Hazlitt, whose observations on human nature are among the keenest ever written, calls our attention to another flaw when he says, "Envy is the most universal passion." Pascal sums it up like this: "We are incapable both of truth and of good."

The tragedy of humanity is seen nowhere more glaringly than in the awful injustices of history. What is history? In no small degree it is a record of "man's inhumanity to man." From Cain and Abel to the prophets and their assassins, from the crucifiers of Jesus to twentieth-century tyrants, brutality and meanness have broken through the cages of this common humanity.

Lord Acton said that nearly all great men were bad men. The German thinker Hegel has spoken of history as "the slaughter-bench at which the happiness of peoples, the wisdom of states, and the virtue of individuals have been victimized." The streams of history are red with the blood of people. The story of Diogenes (412–323 B.C.) going about in broad daylight with a lantern looking for an honest person is painfully relevant in every generation.

No wonder the bitterest words of all languages have been written against human beings. History has been well called the "despair of philosophy."

Several years ago, before a large group of philosophers at a plenary session of the American Philosophical Association, I heard a Harvard professor of philosophy say, "If God is, I would expect him to take an unexcited view of man."

Where, then, is the glory of these human creatures? Are they not rather miserable creatures, worthless and vile?

Again there is nothing new in such a pessimistic thought. For the ancient psalmist was familiar with it when he said:

> They have all gone astray, they are all alike perverse;
>   there is no one who does good,
>   no, not one. (Psalm 14:3)

II. JESUS' VIEW OF PEOPLE

Since we take Jesus seriously, we must turn across the centuries two thousand years to see what he had to say about people. He knew their weaknesses. He was not blind to their sins. Yet he saw in them creatures of unutterable worth.

Little children shone like precious jewels before him. He loved the poor, the maimed, the halt, the blind, the lepers, the sinners, as well as the rich, the healthy, the "righteous." His earthly mission was "to serve, and to give his life a ransom for many"

(Matthew 20:28). He said, "For what will it profit them if they gain the whole world but forfeit their life? Or what will they give in return for their life?" (Matthew 16:26). He who girded himself with a towel and washed his disciples' feet knew the worth of each person (John 13:1-11). He who lamented over Jerusalem so many times (Matthew 23:37) still felt the importance of those who crucified him. He who was called a winebibber and a glutton saw the image of God in the heart of every sinner. He who told the story of the lost sheep had a deep sense of the preciousness of every human being.

How are we to fit these two facts together? On the one hand, it seems that people are not worth much. On the other hand, Jesus, the Savior of the world, tells us that each person is precious in the sight of God. Was Jesus a mere dreamer? Much depends on the answer to this question. We United Methodists join Christians everywhere in looking to Jesus Christ as our Lord and teacher. So with him we affirm the dignity and preciousness of each human being.

How are we to think this through?

III. THE IMAGE OF GOD

We can think it through by answering the question: What does the Bible mean when it says that we are made in God's image? Here we must look for a comprehensive answer based on the primal fact that God created us to bear some real marks of kinship with himself.

The Bible loses its glory if we are of no special value. The mighty thought of God's redemptive love in Jesus Christ means nothing if we are worthless. Where is the victory of the empty tomb if we are mere particles of dust?

Lift up this doctrine that we are made after God's own likeness, however; and we can speak of every person as one "for whom Christ died" (1 Corinthians 8:11). Let us look at this great belief about ourselves in the light of our modern setting.

First of all, here is where we need to stop thinking about our bodies and start thinking about souls. The body is physical, but the soul is spiritual. In spite of what some people may say, a human being is a living spirit.

The Bible teaches us that God is the infinite Spirit. God created us spiritual beings, in the likeness of God. Nobody has ever seen the soul. If the stark truth were told, a congregation or assembly of people is a group of invisible spirits. They have bodies; but their real selves, their souls, are spirits.

The soul is something that no eye can see, no hand can touch, no weight can lift, and no device can measure. How big is a soul? We can never answer that question in inches or feet or miles or light years. In contrast to the vast stretches of things in space, we are like the Maker of this universe, invisible beings who will never be seen through a telescope nor expressed in a mathematical formula. We are creatures of dignity because God made us living spirits.

Much more than that needs to be said. Look at the wonderful powers that people have. Think of the great things people have done.

The wisest and best men and women have always said that there is a difference between what is good and what is bad. They have said that there is a difference between the beautiful and the ugly, the true and the false, the holy and the blasphemous. They have insisted that we are creatures of dignity because we can grow and adventure in things that are good and beautiful and true and holy.

What is the difference between a child and a little monkey? When a monkey gets to be six years old, would we send it to school? Of course not. Why not? Because the monkey cannot really grow in understanding. Can a monkey sing songs or grasp the Ten Commandments or pray to God? Of course not. The monkey is not made in the image of God, but we are.

We are by nature capable of responding to the beautiful. We can love the truth and repudiate errors. We can seek that absolute righteousness that comes only from loyal service to the one true God. In our natural state these capacities are undeveloped and even twisted by our pride and pettiness. Yet they are always there just the same. Because of these things we are creatures of dignity. From this it is only a step to the thought that people are dear to the very heart of God. Even newborn babes are unutterably precious because they belong to God and are made for growth under God.

Children begin their deeds of goodness, perhaps, by sharing a stick of chewing gum and end by sharing their lives in the struggle for truth, love, and justice. They set out by enjoying their colorful little toys and continue until they appreciate Shakespeare and compose symphonies. They commence with Walt Disney's Pluto only to grow until they rethink the thoughts of Plato. They start with a simple bedtime prayer, "Now I lay me down to sleep," only to move on toward an ever-deepening understanding of our Lord's Prayer.

Yet we do not reach the summit of the matter until at last we express ourselves in the language of the saints. The Bible gives us the highest insight here. In it we know God as the one in whom goodness, beauty, truth, and holiness live and have their being. What is goodness but an abstraction until it has its reality in God who is "the good of all good"? What is beauty but a dream until it is clothed in the ultimate mind? What is truth but a word until it speaks through the "God of truth"? What is righteousness but an ideal until it comes to life in the goodness of God?

So when we say that we were created in the image of God, we mean that we were given the power of growing and adventuring, with God's help, in those qualities that belong to God.

Now we begin to see something of the wonder of this doctrine of the "image of God." God is the ultimate Spirit. We are finite spirits. God is infinite goodness. We share in that goodness. God is absolute beauty. We long for beauty. God is holy. We are made for "inward holiness that leads to outward holiness."

Kant (1724–804) said that we are creatures of dignity because we are bearers of the moral law. Even more than that grand insight, we are creatures of dignity because we are bearers of the grace of God.

In the light of this, our reason for living becomes clear. We are made to be children of God. The purpose of life on this earth is, with God's help, to weave into the fabric of a passing existence those qualities that are neither new nor old but everlasting because they come from God.

We United Methodists believe that we are made to be God's children and to belong in God's family. Our natural make-up, which gives us dignity, starts us on the way to God. That by itself, however, is utterly inadequate. Here is where God's special help comes in. We call this the grace of God. By God's grace we, the children of God in promise, become the children of God in fact. The Father loves us with an everlasting love. That is the deeper meaning of the coming of Jesus Christ into the world.

IV. SUMMARY AND PRACTICAL IMPLICATIONS

Why do we believe in the incalculable preciousness of each human being? Because the Bible teaches that God created all people to be the children of God with the mysterious ties of a special kinship. We believe this also because Jesus emphasized it and gave it new depth and meaning, for Christ died for us. We believe it because human beings show in their own lives and activities the marks of God's creative work; for they are capable of growing in goodness, beauty, truth, and holiness. We believe it also because God has wrought a great work in Jesus Christ precisely for the redemption and creative advance of human beings. We believe it because the Holy Spirit does his work in all who respond. We believe it because of the destiny beyond death to which all of us are summoned.

The practical implications of all this need to be noted. If what we believe about the dignity and incalculable preciousness of each human being is important, then no one is to be evaluated on any other basis than the love of God as revealed in Jesus Christ. This means that neither race, nor culture, nor sex, nor age, nor status, nor any other historical or human factor is to obscure the sense of the ultimate worth of people. All are made for God. Christ lived and died for all. The Holy Spirit ever takes the initiative to bless and enrich the lives of all. In the realm of ideal values our paltry human distinctions have no standing before God. All may manifest goodness, beauty, truth, and holiness. For these are not cooped up in any nation, culture, race, sex, or age.

This is one of the primal sources of the United Methodist opposition to everything that dehumanizes people. It is an equally primal source of our passion to improve the lot of all, including especially those in greatest need. It is the reason why we feel called to engage in the endless warfare against ignorance, poverty, injustice, and inhumanity.

CHAPTER 7

We Believe in the Cross

WE ARE CREATURES of dignity, yet we cannot answer our own deepest questions. The cross of Christ must always be seen against the background of our preciousness and of our failure. We were important enough and needy enough for Christ to die for us.

I. OUR THIRST FOR GOD

Someone has said that we are religious creatures. We are. But why? Why have people of all ages turned to the supernatural for help.

The answer is not simple, but it is clear. Whether we look at the crude gropings of primitive peoples or at the refined frustrations of our modern day, we observe that one universal human longing has driven people to worship God. What is that? It is the longing for an enduring meaning in the face of sin and death.

Why did people of all ages long for this enduring meaning? Because they were made for God. People are restless until they rest in God. How do they come to see this momentous fact about themselves? By seeing the failure of everything but God.

1. The Failure of Nature

Primitive people saw clearly that somehow nature was not always their friend. It involved them in disease. It struck them down by droughts and floods and terrifying storms. It threatened them with wild beasts. It always seemed to destroy them in the end.

Today, despite all our scientific conquests of nature—for which daily we thank God—we still look out on a physical universe that threatens our life and all that we hold most dear. Oh, we do not live in the tiny little world of our primitive ancestors. We can travel in outer space and look through telescopes at galaxies even deeper in space. But do we feel more at home in such a universe?

We are told that there are a hundred billion stars in our galaxy. They tell us also that there may be a hundred billion other galaxies the size of ours. Does that make us feel any safer as we face the facts of sin and death? Of course not. Why? Because neither the stars above us nor the earth beneath us can speak to us as person to person. So religion, on its human side, is the longing for communion that breaks through the terrible silence of the universe around us. On its divine side it is God speaking to us and calling us to look beyond nature to the supernatural realm.

Nature is that realm of reality that we know through our senses. We can see it, touch it, smell it, and so forth. Beyond nature there is the supernatural realm. This is not the realm of the superstitious, the ignorant, and the cranky. Rather, it is the realm of ideas, of justice, of love, of grace, of prayer, of worship, of the cross and the kingdom of God. We know that only by turning to God's love can we find the answers to the questions of life and death and destiny.

2. The Failure of Human Beings

Again, people have looked at human history and found it helpless to answer the ageless problems of sin and death. It is true that primitive peoples never had the advantages of reading books. Yet they saw people come and go. They knew human tragedy. They understood premature death and helpless old age. In the passing of the years they were acquainted with the awful tragedy of our inhumanity.

In modern times we can read books and look back across the long centuries. We can follow the slow painful steps that people took to get out of the jungle. But can we find there the meaning of life in the face of sin and death? We cannot. Why not? Because human history pardons no sins and does not conquer death. It merely pictures the long procession of sinners and the endless stream of death. Culture and civilization have failed us also.

3. The Failure of Ourselves

Where shall we turn then? Shall we look into our own souls? What good will that do? It is our souls that demand the answer that they cannot give themselves. The plain fact is that we are driven beyond ourselves, beyond all else, to God.

In the face of our utter inability to cope with our own situation, we long for God. Some people express this longing in the crude language of idol worship, some in the superstitious tongues of painful rites. Always there is the craving for a fellowship with God that can conquer the terror or inadequacy of all earthly attachments.

Lost in the world around us, lost in the dark corridors of history and culture, and lost in ourselves, we thirst for God.

II. GOD'S ETERNAL ANSWER

Then a strange thing happens. We finally begin to see that God wants to speak to us. Abraham saw this. He heard something of the divine speech. Then there was Isaac, then Jacob. Moses stood before God and heard God's voice. The prophets heard the word of God, the message of hope and promise. Finally God saw that the time was ripe for speaking in a way that every human being could understand. So, in Jesus Christ, God spoke in the language of our common humanity. In Christ we know that sin and death are defeated. In the Savior, therefore, we learn to feel at home in this present world. Why? Because through Christ we know that back of this universe there is the heart of God that broke on Calvary.

We United Methodists join all Christians in affirming that God redeemed everyone in the Savior. So we speak of the atoning work of God in Jesus Christ. At the heart of Christianity is the Atonement. What does that mean? It means God's meeting us and drawing us to himself. It means that in the face of sin, which separates us from God, there is a complete forgiveness, which binds us to God. It means that in the face of death, which destroys us, there is God's mighty love, which gives us everlasting life. So nothing can separate us from the love of God in Christ (Romans 8:35-39).

How do we know all this? We know it because God has revealed it in the Bible. We know it by kneeling at the foot of the cross and there beholding the divine method of dealing with sin and death. For the whole story of God's redeeming love centers in the crucified Savior of the world.

III. THE MEANING OF THE CROSS

What does the cross mean?

The church has never reached a final statement about it because no creed can tell the full story. Paul gave the finest single utterance about the cross's meaning when he said, "In Christ God was reconciling the world to himself" (2 Corinthians 5:19). What are the divine redemptive facts here?

1. The Divine Initiative

The first and greatest fact is that God in Christ took the initiative in our behalf. Long in advance God saw our human need. God loved us first. This fact is supremely seen in the cross. As Paul put it, "But God proves his love for us in that while we still were sinners Christ died for us" (Romans 5:8). If this will not draw us to God, nothing will.

2. God Takes Sin Seriously

The second redemptive fact about the cross is that God takes our sin seriously. If God had a trifling attitude toward sin, we would be left unmoved. When we look up at the crucified Christ and see the heart of God broken because of our sin, we get a vision of the awfulness of our failure. Sin breaks the heart of God. When we know this, we are moved to a repentance that binds us to God's forgiving love.

3. Only God Can Save

The third mighty fact about the cross is that God alone can answer the problems of sin and death. The cross means that God has entered into our common humanity to do for us what we could not do for ourselves. This fact moves us to walk with confidence into the presence of God. For we know that God alone can answer our need, and we know also that God wants more than anything to do it.

4. No Limit to God's Love

The fourth divine fact about the cross is that there are no lengths to which God will not go in our behalf. Love can never reach higher than the cross. Nor can it probe deeper. The cross means that God withheld nothing when God gave the Son to die. Since this fact was placed in history on Calvary's hill by the sign of the cross, all people everywhere can know beyond the slightest doubt that, *as far as God is concerned, the way to God is always wide open.* The only obstacle, then, to our entrance into the joys of eternal life now is within our own selves. For the cross is the ageless sign of God's unfaltering readiness to forgive and to bind us to himself.

5. God Suffers to Give Life

The fifth redemptive fact about the cross is that our salvation is always made available at the price of God's suffering. This is what Christians have called *vicarious suffering.* It means that God took on the sufferings of our common humanity for the purpose of lifting us up. Wherever we sin, God suffers. Wherever we are bereaved or lonely or misunderstood, God shares in our sorrow. Jesus did not offer the world some clever remarks about looking to the beautiful, for he had to be about God's business. He knew that life was not that simple. There are hurts to be healed, broken hearts to be comforted, sinners to be forgiven, and fears to be conquered. God, far from serenely contemplating the good, chose to become flesh and blood and took on our pain and suffering. The cross was this perfect, self-giving, suffering love of God in our behalf. When we come to Christ, the crucified Savior, we know that God has done the great redemptive work for us.

6. The Cross: Yesterday, Today, Forever

The last divine fact about the cross to be mentioned here is that God was, is, and ever shall be as revealed in the Christ of the cross (Hebrews 13:8). Calvary was not new to God. It expressed the heart of God. As soon as there were sinners, hearts that broke, and souls that despaired, God's great heart knew the cross that was from the beginning within himself. This has been beautifully expressed in the Book of Revelation, where we read of the Lamb slain from the foundation of the world (Revelation 13:8). The cross is ever present in the heart of God. The Crucifixion is daily reenacted whenever sin and sadness flourish. This too fills us with godly sorrow and pulls us mightily into the marvelous fellowship with God.

IV. THE CROSS IN SACRAMENT AND WORSHIP

The cross is at the heart of Christianity because it is in the heart of God. Our worship centers focus on it. Our stained-glass windows portray it. Our prayers give thanks for it. Our hymns glory in it. Our pulpits proclaim it. Our private meditations concentrate on it. The deeds of all true Christians reflect it.

Central in our worship is the sacrament of Holy Communion. Here United Methodists come together around the Lord's Table to remember what Jesus Christ did on the cross. We remember his sacrifice for us. We remember—what Christians through the centuries have affirmed—that on the cross God has acted mightily in Jesus Christ that we might be forgiven, re-created, and called to the life of unselfish service. As Paul said, "For I handed on to you as of first importance what I in turn had received: that Christ died for our sins in accordance with the scriptures" (1 Corinthians 15:3).

This sacrament is more than a remembrance. For, when entered into in the spirit of honest repentance and faith, it means the recovery of the sense of the presence of God in community. It means that through those Christian symbols of bread and cup—signifying the broken body and the shed blood of our Lord—we are assisted by the mysterious power of the Holy Spirit at work in the community of prayer and faith to be renewed in Christ. Therefore, the sacrament of the Lord's Supper is an occasion of profound meaning and magnificent celebration. For God has acted in our behalf to redeem and remake us for creative living. It is also an occasion when the whole community of Christ hears again Christ's call to shed abroad his light in the world by responsible living in society.

We believe in the cross.

CHAPTER 8

We Believe in the Forgiveness of Sins

THE DOCTRINE OF the forgiveness of our sins is one of the most triumphant notes in the scale of the Christian religion. The Bible sings when it assures us of God's forgiving grace. The Old Testament proclaims it. (See Isaiah 1:18; Psalm 103:12.) The sweetest strains of this note are not heard, however, until we reach the New Testament, where Paul sings: "There is therefore now no condemnation for those who are in Christ Jesus" (Romans 8:1).

I. THE FACT OF SIN

In our day, however, this talk of sin and forgiveness has for many people a strange sound. It seems unrelated to life.

Do we have complexes? Yes. Are there frustrations? Of course. What about fears and resentments? To be sure. Negative thinking? Obviously. Neuroses? Clearly. A chronic sense of futility and ineffectiveness? Yes. What about sin? Here we hesitate. Yet we need not. Call it by what name we will, sin is still with us.

We live in an age of easy excuses. The old and chronic habit of making excuses for ourselves has reached its peak in our time. Why? Because by misusing the honored name of science we can "explain" everything we do.

We easily explain what we do by our biological heritage or by our environment or by reference to subconscious processes. When we get through making these excuses, we end up without facing the most real fact about ourselves—namely, that God made us responsible beings. Yes, ours is an age of clever alibis.

Yet life has a way of puncturing our vain imaginings. For

everyone knows that ungovernable anger is a sure mark of failure. Everyone knows that resentment is not merely the strange product of the environment; it is the evil fruit of a defective character.

Some time ago I saw a cartoon picturing a scene on a playground at a public school. A little boy had hit another over the head with a baseball bat. Two teachers were discussing it. One teacher said to the other in the presence of the culprit, "Now, we must be very careful not to make him feel guilty."

No worse insult can be leveled against human beings than that of excusing them from their responsibility for injuring another. There is no surer sign of mental health than that of feeling guilty when we are guilty.

Our nation and our world are threatened by sin and moral decay. The hopes of freedom are frustrated by sin. We live in a society wherein billions of dollars are spent each year on illegal transactions of one sort or another. Drunkenness is a formidable problem. Drug use and drug addiction are widespread evils. Transient sex and promiscuity are casually condoned. Divorce is a terrible blight on our nation. Racial prejudice thrives in the minds of many. Tyrants still beat people down with their fists both at home and abroad. The threat of nuclear destruction lurks in the background of international affairs. Petty bickerings at home do their deadly work. Our complacent refusals to support the decent causes of our churches and communities shut us out of the kingdom of God.

While we believe that there is good in everyone, we believe also that people are naturally "inclined to evil, and that continually" (see the Articles of Religion, VII).

We neglect God for a "paradise of dainty devices." We defy God by carrying out our own selfish ambitions.

Sin, then, is a fact. Look within and we find it. Look about and there it is. It may take the form of a deed done. Every time we look down the corridors of our memory, there it hangs like a hideous picture on the wall. We tremble before it. We long for pardon.

Sin may be the disposition or set of the soul away from God. We are sinners, whether we commit any specific acts of evil or not, whenever our hearts are not moving with God. Hence, it is of no help to say, "What evil have I done?"

Sin may take the form of a vague sense of wrongness. We want a better life, but we do not live it. Therefore, we say with Paul, "I do not understand my own actions. For I do not do what I want, but I do the very thing I hate" (Romans 7:15).

II. THE ANSWER: GOD'S FORGIVING GRACE

What is the answer?

The first part of the answer is found in the forgiving grace of God that is ours through faith. Two thousand years of Christian history carry us back to the cross, where God's forgiving love is ours for the asking.

We are always trying to save ourselves by trusting in our own devices or by forgetting our sin in good works. But we soon find that we have not come to grips with the inner problem. Even after we have done our very best, we have only done what we should have done anyway. Our sin remains.

Not all our deeds together can deliver us, for what we need is to be brought into a living fellowship with God. This is not done by piling one deed on another. It happens by being honest with God and by accepting in faith the free gift of God's forgiving love in Jesus Christ. "For by grace you have been saved through faith, and this is not your own doing; it is the gift of God" (Ephesians 2:8).

Our part is to recognize our sin before God—which is repentance—and to trust wholly in God's forgiving love—which is faith. God wants to forgive us. That is why Jesus said, "It is your Father's good pleasure to give you the kingdom" (Luke 12:32).

We believe that our sin drives us beyond every human answer to the salvation that comes from God. It is only as we go to a hill outside the walls of Jerusalem that we can kneel and behold, in humble faith, the Savior of the world. Here is where we find the principle of forgiveness—not by culture and politeness, not by information and skills, not by good works, but by God's love are we forgiven. Those other factors have their useful roles in the Christian life. But we are justified only by God's boundless forgiving love in Christ.

III. JUSTIFICATION BY FAITH

We know this from Christian experience. All Christians can sing in their hearts each day the sublime story of forgiveness when God has done this great redemptive work. No wonder Christians compose hymns! They have something to sing about. No wonder they take the good news with them wherever they go! No wonder they want to live for the glory of God and the service of others!

Saul of Tarsus tried to find his way to God by climbing the endless stairway of religious rules. He went and did not arrive. He sought and did not find. At last he began to see the light on the road to Damascus and to know that he was forgiven and loved by the Savior.

That is why, on his first missionary journey at Antioch of Pisidia, Paul could preach the gospel of forgiveness as he did. We can almost see him standing before the crowd in the synagogue there and saying, "Let it be known to you therefore, my brothers, that through this man [Jesus] forgiveness of sins is proclaimed to you; by this Jesus everyone who believes is set free from all those sins from which you could not be freed by the law of Moses" (Acts 13:38-39).

Along this line he wrote to the Galatians, "A person is justified not by the works of the law but through faith in Jesus Christ" (Galatians 2:16).

This new principle of deliverance from sin was like music in the ears of multitudes throughout the ancient world. It was heard in Jerusalem, in the cities of Asia Minor and Macedonia, in Athens, in Corinth, and even in Rome.

After many generations of Christians had lived and died under the glow of this redemptive love, many people returned to a system of salvation by works and ceremonies. Then came Martin Luther (1483–1546) to revive the principle of forgiveness by faith and not by works. After the young Luther was stunned by a bolt of lightning, he promised God that he would become a monk. In the monastery he followed the most rigorous disciplines. He studied long hours. He observed in minute detail all the forms and ceremonies. He went to Rome and knelt his way up the sacred stairs there. When he wrote of those experiences, he likened himself to Paul. Just as the apostle had become a Pharisee of the Pharisees, so Luther became a monk of monks.

Yet Luther's efforts did him no good. He became bitter toward God. He despised the word *penitence.* The righteousness of God was dreadful to think about. Then he finally saw God's righteousness in the light of the words, "The one who is righteous will live by faith" (Romans 1:17; see Galatians 3:11). He grasped what Paul had been talking about centuries ago. He was free from the tyranny of his sin. Now he trusted the Savior to do for him what he could never do. He accepted the free gift of God's forgiveness.

We United Methodists join all Christians in believing in the forgiveness of sins by faith.

IV. THE CONTINUING NEED FOR FORGIVENESS

This is an era of the easy conscience. People are not apt to realize how much they need God's forgiving love. Yet we need forgiveness just as much as did our ancient forebears in Galatia, Corinth, and Rome. They read with joy what Paul said about being forgiven by grace through faith.

Whenever we probe beneath the surface of our superficiality, we too know that we have turned from God to our own ways. We have missed the purpose for which God created us and hence repudiated the reason for our being here. The ancient evils are still with us and at work in us. Hatred, war, prejudice, crime, the breakdown of character, greed, lust, dishonesty, meanness, pettiness, mediocrity—these and many other evils are with us because we are the kind of people we are. We need to be forgiven.

We today, with our limitless powers of self-deception, imagine that we can find our way without repentance and without God's forgiving grace. When we come toward the threshold of religion, we want to substitute the word *acceptance* for *forgiveness.* We want to think that God accepts us as we are, whether or not we are willing to repent. This is neither true to the Bible nor to life. It is a cheap and unrealistic substitute for honest repentance and a living faith. God always loves us. God is ever eager to forgive us and accept us. Yet not even God can pardon us unless we put ourselves in a position to be forgiven. Repentance is basic honesty before God.

We moderns imagine that progress is inevitable, that history is automatically redemptive, that the secular world is essentially good, that education alone is the answer, and that everything roots in economics. There are half-truths here mingled with demonic delusions. These delusions, like beautiful bubbles, have fascinated people and then burst into oblivion.

Two world wars, Vietnam, the disasters in the Middle East, the possibility of nuclear destruction, the increase of crime, the breakdown of the responsible management of sexuality, the threats to marriage and family life, the disruptions in education, the depths of the dimensions of racial prejudice, the appeals to emotion and ideologies rather than to reason, the pollution and degradation of nature in country and city—these and a thousand other desperate problems tell us that far more is wrong with the world than we had supposed. There is, as of old, a radical wrongness within the minds and hearts of people. The issue has to do with whether we can survive with any meaning and dignity.

We United Methodists, in this era of humankind's desperate need, are increasingly aware of our failures. At the same time, we are convinced that God, in infinite love and wisdom, has shown the way in Jesus Christ. Repentance and forgiveness through faith are the starting points for all renewal in persons and in cultures. For here is the beginning of integrity before God. This beginning is desperately needed. The issue is one of moral and spiritual survival as against either massive destruction or degeneration into societies of dishonest and mediocre people.

Jesus confronted people in his day with what we need in ours. He was informed by eyewitnesses of those Galileans whose blood Pilate mingled with the sacrifices. Then he said: "Do you think that because these Galileans suffered in this way they were worse sinners than all other Galileans? No, I tell you; but unless you repent, you will all perish just as they did" (Luke 13:1-3).

We believe in the forgiveness of sins.

CHAPTER 9

We Believe in Victory
Through Disciplined Living

IT IS ONE THING to be forgiven; it is another thing to be empowered. The earliest Christians rejoiced not only in God's forgiving love but also in God's empowering grace. This was theirs through disciplined living within the fellowship of believers.

Methodism, as the name implies, shares in this heritage. At first the word *Methodists* was used to make fun of a group of young men at Oxford University, England, for their regularity in Christian living. Among them were John and Charles Wesley. They decided to take their Christianity seriously. They banded themselves together in a program of disciplined living. Because they lived their Christianity by *method,* they were called "Methodists." The name remained to characterize one of the greatest movements in Christian history.

The name *United Methodist* brings together various communities of faith that have shared in this great heritage of disciplined living. We believe in victory through the fulfillment of conditions. Nothing that is basic in the moral and spiritual life happens by chance. We reap what we sow.

We realize the importance of this idea the moment we see ourselves as we really are. There is a lot of good in every one of us. Yet we are not good enough. In fact, we are a strange mixture of good and bad. Nothing is clearer than that we need some method of victorious living.

For example, we need the courage to stand for what is right; and we need to know how to get it. It was my privilege for thirteen years to be associated with Franklin N. Parker of Emory University. Everyone who knew him held him in high regard. He was a great man. I remember how he emphasized the need for Christian courage and how he spoke of it as a rare quality. He was right.

We need patience, self-control, and absolute honesty. We need victory over temptation. Above all, we need love. Here our fine resolutions fail us. We resolve to have done with dishonesty and infidelity, but we fall into the same old ruts. We, therefore, are driven to ask the great questions: How can we live victoriously? How can we be the kind of people we really want to be? How can we be what God wants us to be?

I. THE BIBLE'S PROMISE

The Bible teaches that we are made to be not only conquerors but "more than conquerors through him who loved us" (Romans 8:37). Victory is promised everyone who seeks it in the right way. It is not ours merely because we wish it. Nor does it come to us by hit-and-miss techniques. For there are laws of the spiritual life.

Again and again the Bible reminds us of these laws. We are to "wait," to "watch and pray," to "hold fast," to "press forward." In fact we are to become spiritual athletes (1 Corinthians 9:24).

The Bible encourages us with its great promises.

> Even youths will faint and be weary,
>   and the young will fall exhausted;
> but those who wait for the LORD shall renew their
>   strength,
>   they shall mount up with wings like eagles,
> they shall run and not be weary,
>   they shall walk and not faint (Isaiah 40:30-31).

Those who hunger and thirst for righteousness shall be filled (Matthew 5:6). The pure in heart shall see God (Matthew 5:8). "Ask, and it will be given you; search, and you will find; knock, and the door will be opened for you" (Matthew 7:7). When Jesus said, "Ask," he did not mean, "Inquire a little." When he said "Search," he did not mean, "Look around a little." When he said "Knock," he did not mean, "Tap." The Master was talking about a passionate, persistent, and sensible searching.

But we cannot realize these promises unless we first come to grips with some of the enemies of Christ that work within us every day.

II. A MAJOR OBSTACLE TO VICTORIOUS LIVING

What are the greatest enemies of victorious Christian living? People of equal wisdom might say different things. I believe that the worst enemies from within are these: *distraction* and *self-love.*

Put it like this. Who are we? We are our thoughts and our desires. We are more than these, but we find the key to ourselves in the quality of what we think and what we want. Distraction has to do with our thoughts, while self-love has to do with our desires.

Let us look first at our distracted thoughts and see how they interfere with a vital spiritual life. Here I am talking about something everyone experiences. Yet not everyone realizes what is going on within the soul. By *thoughts* I mean whatever comes into our minds, whether it be the memory of yesterday's pleasures, the fear of tomorrow's problems, the ring of a telephone, the scream of a siren, the throbbing of a headache, or anything else that we are aware of. In the midst of so many things that claim our attention, we forget God; and we forget every promise we ever made to God.

During each waking moment we are thinking of something or other. Like the coming and going of the waves on the ocean, thoughts come and go in our minds. Often without rhyme or reason we swing and sway from thought to thought. Regardless of the quality of these comings and goings within us, we are entertained by them as if by a constant flow of inner television programs. Why? Because, good, bad, or mediocre, they are our very own. Then another day has passed. When we thought last of God we cannot remember.

Is there power in such a day? Of course not. Why not? Because there is not and cannot be power in the mere flow of unrelated thoughts and feelings. Thomas Edison was asked once whether he believed in luck. He replied, "No; and if I did, I'd regard myself as the most unlucky fellow that ever lived. For every one of my inventions came only after a lot of hard work." Then he added, "The only difference between me, who's supposed to be lucky, and other people is that while they think about many different things, I think of one thing until I get what I'm after." This is the key principle in all phases of life. It applies supremely to the spiritual life.

Christ demands unity, but our minds are swallowed up in multiplicity. This is one of the great battlefields of the soul. Mediocre thoughts and feelings, however entertaining, add up to a mediocre person. For as a person "thinketh in his heart, so is he" (Proverbs 23:7, KJV). As life goes on, few things take us nearer to the brink of hell than the realization that our one chance to live on earth was spent on a vast and meaningless assortment of trifles.

Ours is an age of mediocrity because, more than any other, it is the age of distraction. For example, our forebears had the Bible and a few other books. They could fix their minds on those few things. We have so many books that we do not know what to read. With the coming of radio, television, the press, and the Internet, and with the increase of leisure time made possible by machines, computers, and automation, we have reached the point where disciplined living is the only alternative to mediocrity.

The great question is this: How can we escape from this fruitless living, with its endless rounds of triviality and defeat?

III. THE ANSWER

We can almost hear someone say, "The answer is simple: just think about God and the Kingdom all of the time!" But this misses the mark. Why? Because nobody can do it.

Living involves many interests. In order to keep body and soul together, we have to think about many different things. Where is the answer then?

Nearly three thousand years of devotional history show us the way. Isaiah caught a glimpse of the heart-principle of victorious living when he said, "In returning ... you shall be saved" (Isaiah 30:15). We are not made to think of just one thing during the day, for many things crowd in on us. We are made to keep returning to God and the things of God. This is the basis of disciplined Christian living. Why set apart times each day and week for worship? Because in these sacred moments God brings a new and holy beauty to all the rest of life. It is just here that we see the amazing relevance for our distracted age of United Methodism's call to the disciplined life.

IV. ANOTHER OBSTACLE TO VICTORIOUS LIVING

There is another serious threat from within to victorious living. This threat is self-love. Our world revolves around ourselves instead of Christ. If it is true that we are what we think, it is also true that we are what we want. (See Matthew 6:21.)

Christ demands the love of God and others, but naturally and easily we love ourselves. This shuts out God. To be sure, up to a point, we are supposed to love ourselves. Jesus knew this when he said, "You shall love ... your neighbor as yourself" (Luke 10:27). But the tragedy of life is that we are so fascinated with our own beloved selves that we miss the glorious life of service in the kingdom of God.

Now and then everyone wants to go all out in this kind of unselfish service to God and humankind. In rare moments we feel like Peter when he said to Jesus, "Though all become deserters because of you, I will never desert you" (Matthew 26:33). Yet Jesus knew that on that very night this impetuous disciple would deny him. We too are like Peter. Why? Because we keep returning to our self-love until it overrules our noblest impulses. Our highest resolutions are often broken at last on the hard rock of our selfishness and greed.

Besides this, our self-love pulls us in a thousand directions. In one moment it lures us toward money, in another toward social position, in another toward revenge, and in yet another toward companionship. Self-love compels us to take advantage of our fellows and at the same time to seek their praise. It tries to justify every kind of folly. It passionately craves social status, and yet it uses the tongue to cut others down. Self-love seeks peace and promotes conflict. It drives people through the wild rounds of pleasure, and it plunges them into the deep and lonely pools of remorse. The fact is that self-love is a chaos of conflicting desires.

It leaves us where Peter the Great of Russia found himself when he said, "I wish to reform my empire, but I cannot reform myself."

The pity of it is that the work of this self-love goes on so close to us, and so pleasantly within us, that we do not realize what has been happening until we get a vision of Christ and behold the decent, honest, loyal, unselfish persons we might have been.

V. THE ANSWER

Here again, we United Methodists find the answer in the heart-principle of nearly three thousand years of devotional experience: "In returning ... you shall be saved."

To what are we to return in order to overcome the gravitational pull of our self-love? We are to return to God and the things of God, to Christ and his love, to the great passages of the Bible, to the family altar, to private devotions and honest living, to public worship, to prayer and study, to good books and creative fellowship. We are to become dynamically incorporated into the community of prayer and faith. Life is not improved by accident. Nor is it sustained in goodness by chance. For God works mightily through the Christian habits to bless us and others through us.

Through the habits of Christian devotion God gives us the power of living daily under the inspiration of our highest and holiest moments, and God gives the power that comes from a complete commitment. Through discipline God opens the great passages of the Bible until the soul finds the element for which it was created—the love of God and our fellow human beings.

We United Methodists need to recover in this age the grand disciplines of the spiritual life that are so vital a part of our heritage. When it is time to study our Sunday school lesson, we are to do it—television program or no television program—for we are to understand what the Bible is all about. When the doors of the church are open, we are to be there. When asked to serve, we are to see the high privilege of it and respond accordingly. When asked to give, we are to do it joyfully and liberally. We are to pray, just as Jesus prayed, at regular times and to celebrate the sacrament of the Lord's Supper with joy and rededication.

How do we gain victory? By proven methods.

I love the mountains. I like to see them when the morning sun wakes them up with a kiss on their brows. I like to see them in the evening when, like sleeping giants, they lie tucked away under the cover of darkness. Yet I look out of my study window and do not see the mountains. Why not? Because I have not put myself in a position to see them. So is it with us and God.

CHAPTER 10

We Believe in the Centrality of Love

CHRISTIAN LOVE HAS been rightly called the greatest thing in the world, for it binds us to God and to others. It is the law of life because it fulfills every law (Romans 13:8-10; Galatians 5:14). Without it we do not really live; we merely exist. The supreme reason for exalting Jesus Christ as Lord is that he perfectly embodies the love of God.

I. JESUS' EMPHASIS ON LOVE

Jesus showed us, once and for all, that love is the basic principle of human relations. He taught that God is love and introduced the world to love as a creative dynamic power. This principle of living was new. To be sure, there was the ancient commandment, "You shall love your neighbor as yourself" (Leviticus 19:18). Jesus carried it far beyond anything that went before him by showing what it really means to be a neighbor. (See Luke 10:25-37.)

One could obey the law of loving neighbor as self and still hate the Samaritan, but Jesus took a despised Samaritan and made him the hero of one of the world's most beautiful stories. One could love neighbor as self and still have a low concept of women. Jesus gave to women their rightful place. One could love neighbor as self and abhor sinners. Jesus taught the love of sinners. One could love neighbor as self and hate one's enemies. Jesus said, "Love your enemies and pray for those who persecute you, so that you may be children of your Father in heaven" (Matthew 5:44-45).

More than teaching this love, Jesus lived it. He who taught that we should be concerned about the outcasts loved the hated Samaritans (John 4:7-42) and was even accused of being one of them (John 8:48). He who asked his disciples to love sinners was condemned for being a friend of tax collectors and sinners (Luke 7:34). He who said, "Love your enemies," prayed, while hanging on the cross, "Father, forgive them; for they do not know what they are doing" (Luke 23:34).

Jesus unveiled the heart of God and revealed the only principle of life that has the Creator's sanction. He showed us with absolute finality that without the love of God no life can stand and with that love no life can fail. In contrast to the proud person's boast and the tyrant's fist, the love of Christ abides forever. That love becomes the governing power of the new humanity in Christ.

For this reason Jesus gave his disciples the new commandment.

II. PAUL SPEAKS OF LOVE

It is also fascinating to see how this stress on love pervaded the thinking of the first Christians. They had their disagreements. (See for example Galatians 2:11.) They knew the difficulties of working together. Yet they labored under the inspiration of a common affection.

Paul, the apostle of faith, could even more fittingly be called the apostle of love. His great words on love in the thirteenth chapter of First Corinthians are unrivaled in all literature on that subject both for their beauty and for their practical sanity. As every Christian knows, love heads the list of the Christian virtues.

It is not often realized that Paul placed his magnificent words on love in the context of his remarks on the essential unity of Christians. There are things that divide people. Some have special gifts. Yet there is one baptism and one Spirit (1 Corinthians 12:13). There is one body with many members. The central reality of the Christian community is not prophecy, miracles, healing, speaking in tongues, and so forth. Paul challenges us to desire the higher gifts and then shows us "a still more excellent way" (1 Corinthians 12:31).

He tells us that we may speak with the tongues of angels, which would be a wonderful thing, but without love we would be "a noisy gong or a clanging cymbal." We may have prophetic powers, of which many today are boasting. We may understand every mystery and have all knowledge, which would be an unbelievably great advantage. We may have all faith so as to remove mountains, which means that we could say to any mountain in our way, "Move! Be gone!" Yet, says Paul, if we have all these powers and do not have love, we are nothing. Then he tells us what love is and how it acts. After speaking of the things that are sure to fail, he tells of the things that abide: faith, hope, and love; "and the greatest of these is love" (1 Corinthians 13:13).

III. WHAT IS LOVE?

We United Methodists believe in the life of love. What is Christian love? Some people think of it as a weak, sentimental, gushy feeling that has nothing to do with love. They view it as a kind of sweet agreeableness that prides itself on going along with people no matter what they do. This is not Christian love. For sometimes love is firm. Jesus was not only "meek and mild." He was also stern. When he cleansed the Temple, driving out the merchants and overturning the tables of the money changers, he was not trying to be a "good fellow" (John 2:14-16). He was not meek and mild when he called Herod a fox (Luke 13:32); nor was he gentle when he identified Peter with Satan (Matthew 16:23). He was not a weak and "pale Galilean" when he confronted the Pharisees with his blistering "Woe to you ... hypocrites!" (Matthew 23:13-36).

A balance is needed here. What, then, is Christian love? Within the fellowship of the redeemed, it means the eager concern to do God's work together in the church. It means the desire to bear our part of the load and at the same time to bear the burdens of others. Outside the fellowship, love is the burning passion for God's best for everyone in the world. It knows no barriers and withholds itself from no one. Christian love does not seek its own way, for it is God's way. It wants to feed the hungry; to clothe the naked; to welcome the stranger; to visit and heal the sick; to lift up the fallen; and, above all, to draw every human being into the orbit of the love of God in Jesus Christ. Its nature is to share. Its opposite is to withhold. Its genius is to show no partiality.

To have Christian love does not mean to like all people equally. Doing that is impossible. It means rather to want God's best for all people regardless of our likes and dislikes. It means doing what we can where and when we can.

IV. LOVE IN TODAY'S WORLD

The world is hungry, naked, sick, lonely; it is war-torn, drug-saturated, and weary; it is bitter, petty, and mean. It has drifted far from the great Creator's love. How can the world's needs be met? Only by the mighty power of a self-denying love. Christian love means the cross. It means the fellowship and privilege of suffering in behalf of others.

The suffering peoples of the world and the downtrodden find in Christ their champion, for he lived and died for them. Every Christian is called, with Timothy, to take his or her "share in suffering like a good soldier of Christ Jesus" (2 Timothy 2:3). Out of the love of Christ the ignorant are to be taught, the weak encouraged, the bewildered guided, and the lost brought back into the fold. This love of Christ is a mighty thing. It works through consecrated individuals. It works even more through the cooperative adventures of those who are in the fellowship of believers. It makes for peace, seeks justice, and encourages creativity.

The stark truth is that after two thousand years we are beginning to see, as a world, that we are engaged in a race between the love of Christ and world disaster. God's love, as it is in Christ, fits the world's need today. Let all Christians who are entering the twenty-first century wake up together to the ministry of compassion! For this is the will of God in Christ Jesus.

V. LOVE IN SOLITARY SOULS

When we turn from the world to our own individual souls, we see also how perfectly this love of Christ fits our need. In personal living, only love will work.

There never was an age when so many people had the time and money for the luxury of analyzing their own frustrations. Everywhere, we meet those who know what is wrong with themselves but who are powerless to do anything about it. Ever thinking about living, they never quite get around to it. They look into each nook and cranny of their minds and dissect every impulse. They long for and need a sympathetic listener. The pity of their lives is that they do everything except the one thing that is needful. They do not give themselves in a magnificent abandon to the service of God and others. They withhold themselves from their share of unselfish suffering.

We are engaged in a colossal search for our identity. We want to know who we are. This is important, but the question is this: Can we find our identity by seeking it? Rather, is it not like true happiness? When we seek it for its own sake, we miss it. Then, under the leadership of Jesus Christ, we open ourselves to some great cause that is incalculably more important than ourselves, and behold, both identity and happiness come our way. "For," said Jesus, "those who want to save their life will lose it, and those who lose their life for my sake, and for the sake of the gospel, will save it" (Mark 8:35).

God did not create our minds to look deeply into themselves. He made them to turn outward on the world in work and helpful service. While it is the rightful job of some to probe deeply into the human spirit, this is not the business of most people. We are to love and work and be thankful for what we are and what we can do.

Any attitude other than love fails. Resentment, whether taken in large doses or small, is poison. Pet peeves get us nowhere. Looking down on people becomes comical in the light of Almighty God. Envy is as useless as it is universal. Suspicion is a thief that robs us of friends. Indifference slowly but surely leads us downhill into the bogs of cynicism. Only love abides. For "God is love" (1 John 4:16b).

VI. LOVE IMPLIES BOTH LAW AND WISDOM

It is often supposed that love can express itself properly with a minimal interest in moral laws and rules. We are told that love alone is absolute. We are told also that we should not hesitate to break any law, moral or otherwise, if the situation seems to call for it. This is basically misguided. To be sure, there is a truth here. Circumstances do alter cases. Yet the deeper truth is that we cannot persistently express love without policies, rules, or moral laws. What is love without a policy of loyalty? What is love without a policy of courtesy? What is love without basic guidelines concerning telling the truth, honesty, mutual respect, the willingness to listen, the eagerness to respond if we can when asked? What is love in a world at war without peacemaking policies? What is love without the desire to improve on ourselves and our competence?

Love also implies wisdom. Love must not be at the mercy of stupidity. It demands resourcefulness. Love has a job to do. How can we know whether the work of love is being done unless we use the minds that God has given us? Authentic love is not blind. Rather, it is guided and informed by the wisdom that God wants us to reflect in all our efforts to express love. Love is the engine; intelligence is the steering wheel. It is not easy to know who does the most harm, the vicious or the mistaken. Here I am not talking about highly sophisticated levels of intellectual understanding. I am talking about what every normal human being has—namely, practical intelligence. The point is that it must be used. For love requires it.

VII. THE CALL TO ALL CHRISTIANS

We United Methodists join all Christians in believing in the new life of love. There is no alternative to it. We are not free to take it or leave it. Jesus Christ commanded it. Life demands it. The grace of God supplies it. Our salvation depends on it. We are saved by faith. We continue to be saved by "faith working through love" (Galatians 5:6).

Both nations and individuals plead for the united efforts of all Christians in a worldwide program of compassion and wisdom based on the love of God. For God will conquer war by the love that works for peace. God will banish ignorance and prejudice by the love that strives for truth. God will build the Kingdom on the love that rejoices in the privilege of service.

Wesley gave us one of the best formulas when he urged his followers to strive for "inward holiness which leads to outward holiness." We United Methodists know that we are sinners redeemed by grace and called to proclaim the power of Christ to change people for the glory of God and the blessing of others.

CHAPTER 11

We Believe in Conversion, Assurance, and Scriptural Holiness

WE BELIEVE IN the new life in Christ. Wesley said that at the moment when God pardons us, God recreates our souls. We are born anew. God also gives us inner assurance, and we are set on our way toward scriptural holiness. While we United Methodists do not say that these affirmations about the Christian life are ours exclusively, we do say that we have a passion to make them burn like divine flames in the hearts of people.

I. WHAT CONVERSION IS AND WHY WE BELIEVE IN IT

We believe in conversion. What is it? It is the most basic transformation in life. It is a revolution at the heart of one's being. It is the new birth. It is not a natural growth but a supernatural rebirth.

For selfish persons, conversion means a basic change in the center of their commitment. Self is dethroned; Christ is enthroned. For those who measure success and failure in dollars and cents, the new birth means the reign of Christ and of his standards. For those who put their highest trust in political organizations and in the might of arms, conversion means seeing in Christ the only hope of the world. To those who are crippled by failure and despair, conversion means absolute trust in the healing ministry of the conquering Savior. In short, we are born of the Spirit when Christ becomes the master impulse of our life. We enter into this new life at the moment when we take all that we know about ourselves and lay it trustfully before all that we know about Christ.

Conversion or the new birth, then, is a basic change of mind and heart. The skeptic may say, "Let's be realistic. People cannot change their identity. They remain themselves. So all this talk about a new being or a new heart doesn't make sense."

Here we need a clear understanding of what we are talking about. In moral and spiritual matters it is of utmost importance to deal in reality and not fantasy. Paul said, "So if anyone is in Christ, there is a new creation; everything old has passed away; see, everything has become new" (2 Corinthians 5:17). How can there be a new creation when people remain themselves? *They can change their direction, their values, and their feelings.* No inherent psychological process prevents this. In fact, both psychology and our general insight into human nature show that this change is possible.

We cannot change our identity as conscious individuals. Nor should we want to do so. In a true sense, we are always ourselves. We keep our names and signatures; but we can alter our aims, accept new standards and values, and change our attitudes and feelings. Moreover, anyone may move from the overwhelming sense of meaninglessness and despair to the awareness of meaning and joy. We can change our vocabulary and our tone of voice; we can make our conversation therapeutic. We can conquer temptations. Rather, with the help of God, we can do these things.

Conversion, or "the new creation" Paul speaks of, means a basic change of purpose, of values, of affections, and of life-meaning wrought by the power of God. If God can help us change our fundamental purpose, God can convert us. If God can help us change our standards and values, our attitudes and our feelings about the meaning of life, then God can convert us. If God can forgive us and help us to know that we are rightly related to God in heart and purpose, God can convert us. Old things have in fact passed away, and all that counts has become new. According to the New Testament, we may experience precisely these things— whether gradually or suddenly—through faith in Jesus Christ.

Why do we believe in conversion?

1. The Bible Affirms It

We believe in conversion because the Bible affirms it. If there is one thing on which the Bible is clear, it is this: *Anyone can begin a new life with God's help.* This truth runs like a theme throughout the Scriptures. From the vision of Jacob at Bethel to the transforming experience of Moses in Midian; from the repentance and faith of David the king to the conversion of Isaiah the prophet; from Matthew the tax collector to Saul the persecutor of Christians—in short, from beginning to end—the Bible is a book about conversion. *Turn, return, forsake, choose—* these words and many others like them are among the most striking in the Bible. They call us to the new life in God.

2. Jesus Taught It

We believe in conversion because Jesus taught it. The story of the prodigal son sums it up for the people who are down and out. They need not stay the way they are (Luke 15:11-32). Jesus did not confine this principle of conversion to those who wandered far from home, however. Nicodemus was a good man. Yet when he came to Jesus by night to inquire about spiritual things, Jesus said to him, "Very truly, I tell you, no one can see the kingdom of God without being born from above" (John 3:3). He too needed the new birth, for there are many ways of missing God. All of us need to be born again. This is what Jesus taught.

3. Christian History Confirms It

We believe in conversion because Christian history confirms it. No fact of recorded history is more securely grounded in the evidence than this one. Take away the fact of conversion, and we cannot account for Christianity. The only reasonable thing here, then, is to accept the witness of people like Paul, Augustine, Wesley, and millions of others who have witnessed to the new birth in Christ.

4. The Facts of Life Require It

We believe in conversion also because the facts of life require it. How do people get changed? The obvious answer is by a gradual process. There is a great truth here. We learn many things little by little. Like the flowers of the field we grow gradually.

Yet there is within each of us another power that does not

operate on the principle of gradualness. Some of our finest thoughts come suddenly. Some of our most crucial decisions occur in high and holy moments. The profoundest transformations may take place in a flash. Often our faith comes in unforgettable moments.

The point is this: *because there is within us not only the power of gradual change but also the power of sudden transformation, God can do this mighty work within us in the twinkling of an eye.* The Holy Spirit often moves swifter than a weaver's shuttle. On our part, preparation for conversion may be slow, uncertain, gradual. Yet conversion itself may be as sudden and sure as decision.

Many people, in the interest of gradualness, postpone what ought to be done *now.* Knowledge comes slowly. Wisdom takes time. Art is long. An unforgiving spirit can be changed in an instant. A new goal in life may be accepted *now.* New values and attitudes may be chosen *now.* A new relationship toward God and others, through forgiveness, may be experienced *now.* A new sense of meaning and destiny—with the summons to start shining in a great work for God—may be awakened *now.*

For many people life is a feverish effort to deal with their evil habits one at a time. They forget something. They forget that it is easier to change our whole person than it is to overcome our degrading habits. They forget that a transformed person means transformed habits. When the Savior gives new life to a human being, new habits are set in motion.

There comes a time when we have to make up our minds about the kind of people we are going to be. If such a time needs to be repeated, let it be repeated. For our commitment must be sealed. We cannot serve God and wealth (Matthew 6:24).

II. ASSURANCE

We believe in assurance. Why?

First of all, because the New Testament affirms it. The sheep within the fold know their shepherd (John 10:5, 14). The Holy Spirit guides the faithful (John 16:13). The Spirit assures them that they belong to God. This is the witness of the Spirit (Romans 8:16).

We believe in assurance also because Christian experience

confirms it. Whatever keeps returning to us in the ongoing of life is the sure test here. As life goes on, we know, with an ever-deepening sense of assurance, that God is with us. Just as children increasingly know that they belong to their earthly parents, so Christians know that they belong to God. Now and then they may have doubts. The continuing state of their souls is that of an unfaltering assurance, however.

We know that God forgives us. We know that God is with us in our daily work. We know that when we are tempted, God helps us to gain the victory. We know that God confirms us as we enter into the community struggles for truth and justice. We know that we never walk alone through the valley of the shadow of death. When we look back across the winding road of life, we know that God has seen us through. We know that the promise of heaven is sure. "Blessed Assurance" is not merely the title of a hymn, it is a state of the soul. It may come and go, but it is real and God has promised it.

Therefore, we United Methodists believe that everyone is entitled to enter into the joy of this experience.

III. SCRIPTURAL HOLINESS

We believe in scriptural holiness. As we have seen, *conversion* is the doorway through which we enter the Christian life. Once in the house of God, we rejoice in the *assurance* that we belong to God. In the nature of the spiritual life we are then to move from room to room and story to story. The new birth starts us off in the crib where, as newborn babes, we partake of the milk of God's Word and grow thereby (1 Peter 2:2). We are confined to the nursery for a time. Gradually, however, we become stronger and learn to walk into the larger rooms of God's house. It is God's good pleasure to see the children of God grow in grace.

Some tell us that just as the new birth comes as the first work of grace, Christian perfection, or sanctification, comes as the second definite work of grace. There is a first story in the house of God; and there is a second story. Some of the finest Christians I have known—both at home and in the church—have experienced scriptural holiness as a second definite work of grace. Perhaps all would agree, however, that we should not limit the house of God to these two stories. Controversies on this topic have gone far into many a night. Much remains to be said. John Wesley has been rightly claimed as a witness on both sides. He *believed* in scriptural holiness as a second definite work of grace because of the testimony of others. In my opinion, he never clearly and unambiguously *professed* it.

This difference of opinion has become one of the most controversial topics in evangelical Christianity, and in many circles it continues to be just that. We need, above all, to see that there are at least six basic points on which we can all agree.

1. In The United Methodist Heritage

The interest in scriptural holiness was a part of the evangelical movement of the eighteenth and nineteenth centuries. Wesley emphasized it because it is a characteristic feature of New Testament teaching. It was partly because of this emphasis that Wesley devoted thirteen of his forty-four standard sermons to the Sermon on the Mount. This led Wesley to instruct his preachers to call every Christian to move on toward perfection. He never said he had attained it. Wesley preached and taught it as God's power to fill the soul with love and purity of intention. The stress on scriptural holiness is therefore a characteristic feature of our United Methodist heritage.

It was no accident that a paragraph on sanctification, though not approved as one of the Articles of Religion, was appended to them when three branches of Methodism came together in 1939 to form The Methodist Church. Nor was it any accident that the Confession of Faith (finally adopted in 1962) of The Evangelical United Brethren Church (formed when the United Brethren in Christ and the Evangelical Church merged in 1946) contains an Article (XI) on "Sanctification and Christian Perfection" with three carefully worded paragraphs. Consequently, there are two statements on sanctification in *The Book of Discipline of The United Methodist Church*.

John Wesley, Martin Boehm, Philip William Otterbein, Francis Asbury, Christian Newcomer, and Jacob Albright—all of whom figure in the heritage of The United Methodist Church—shared, in one way or another, this interest in sanctification and scriptural holiness. There have been differences of opinion on this. Some, in contrast to Wesley's view, have held to the idea of *imputed* righteousness rather than *actual* righteousness.

One of the finest statements I know on this subject is that in the first paragraph of Article XI of the Confession of Faith. It reads as follows:

> We believe sanctification is the work of God's grace through the Word and the Spirit, by which those who have been born again are cleansed from sin in their thoughts, words and acts, and are enabled to live in accordance with God's will, and to strive for holiness without which no one will see the Lord. (*The Book of Discipline* [1996], Paragraph 62, page 67)

We are reminded in that same Article that sanctification "may be received in this life both gradually and instantaneously, and should be sought earnestly by every child of God." Then we are reminded, very appropriately, that this experience does not deliver us from infirmities, ignorance, and the possibility of sin.

We United Methodists believe that this emphasis on sanctity or scriptural holiness has a continuing role of major importance in Christianity. We are aware that it needs to be comprehended in the light of the whole sweep of the biblical revelation. That is, it must be seen as the direction toward which we are summoned in the light of God's revealed purpose to realize moral and spiritual values under Christ in community. No atomistic or sectarian interpretation will do. No obscuring of that sublime divine goal can measure up to what God requires of us. For it is as easy as it is sinful to seek righteousness for its own sake. There is no surer sign of imperfection than the feeling that we need not continue to grow in grace. The true meaning of sanctification or Christian perfection is not in a state but in a sustained direction of life with God. It is a moving where God is moving with God's help. God's grace is sufficient for the greatness of God's call to holiness. What is scriptural holiness? As Wesley said, it is the love of God and neighbor born and nurtured in us by divine grace.

2. The Only Direction

Christian perfection is the only direction in which to move, so United Methodism is congenial to the call of Jesus to be perfect. (See Matthew 5:48.) It is our deep-seated conviction that God's grace is sufficient to make us perfect in love. Just as our commitment can be sure, our sincerity in love can be sustained. United Methodists agree, then, that the grace of God is fully able to work within our hearts to make them pure and loving and increasingly wise. (See 1 Thessalonians 5:23.) It is our earnest prayer that we may be made perfect in love day by day. If United Methodism loses this passion for scriptural holiness, it will not only betray its heritage; it will also neglect its mission in the world. No one is perfect, but everyone is called to move toward perfection.

3. Room For All

We are agreed that everyone who thinks of sanctification as a second definite work of grace is surely at home in the atmosphere of United Methodism. As I have noted, since the earliest days of our history some of the finest Christians profess this second definite work of grace. There is something bracing about the stress on the suddenness and definiteness of the workings of the Holy Spirit. For when we expect nothing in particular to happen, we are not apt to receive anything.

4. More and More Grace

It is also in keeping with the spirit of United Methodism to feel that God leads us from story to story, from experience to experience, in God's great house. We are always to live in the expectation of being led by God to ever higher dimensions of Christian living. No matter who we are or in what stage of Christian development, there is profound truth for us all in the words "he gives all the more grace" (James 4:6). There is no room for boasting here because we are not affirming our own achievements but God's grace. The plain fact is that we need all the help we can get to rise above mediocrity. It does not require the grace of God to be a mediocre person.

5. United in Love

Again, we are all agreed that no United Methodist church should allow its differences over the interpretation of scriptural holiness to be in the least a source of bitterness and strife. For the great principle to remember here is that we are all "one body in Christ" (Romans 12:5; see also 1 Corinthians 12:12-27). Neither ministers nor lay persons can be wise in creating strife that actually nullifies the whole ideal of Christian perfection. We must in love agree to differ. For we know that people are far more important than their particular interpretations of Christian truth. In this way the profound and beautiful longing within us for perfect love can be nurtured. God can have the fullest chance to do God's wonderwork.

6. Sanctity in the Ecumenical Heritage

Finally, this stress on scriptural holiness has placed United Methodists in the main current of Christian history since the days of the apostles. These ancient forebears were concerned about righteous living with God's help. Their stress on the power of the Holy Spirit to lift us up and to enable us to reflect the love of Christ shows this. Moreover, in all the centuries of Christian history there have been those who, following in the line of the apostles, shared in seeking ever greater resources for doing God's work in the world. Wesley and his followers called this the quest for Christian perfection or for scriptural holiness. Some have called it saintliness; others, sanctity or sanctification. The devotional literature of all eras of Christian history discloses this concern. The various streams that converged to form United Methodism have moved in this same direction.

In the modern world there is an awakening of interest in the power of the Spirit to transform and elevate human existence. From the evangelicals who stress sanctification to the Roman Catholics who talk of sanctity, there is this shared quest. We United Methodists believe that God is present in all this.

We are aware of the dangers here of lapsing into a sect-type mentality. For people can be carried away with a kind of spiritism that disconnects itself from tradition, from the historic community, from doctrine, and from ethical responsibility in the world. United Methodism has demonstrated, along with other Christian communities, that this need not be the case.

We continue to believe in scriptural holiness as God's call to us in these times. The divine summons given through Moses must still be heard: "Speak to all the congregation of the people of Israel and say to them: You shall be holy, for I the LORD your God am holy" (Leviticus 19:2).

We are to hear and obey the often unheeded words of our Lord, "Strive first for the kingdom of God and his righteousness" (Matthew 6:33).

CHAPTER 12

We Believe in the Church

THE CHURCH OF Jesus Christ is an institution of utmost importance. Why? Because it proclaims the eternal gospel from generation to generation.

Yet the church has many critics. Like every good force in the world it undergoes its baptism of fire again and again. Some say the church is too superstitious. Others say it disturbs the consciences of people too much. Many say that it does not make its members any different from other people. Some say the church has too much social vision. Others say it has not enough. Still others tell us that it is divided into too many parts. Then there are always those who lie in bed on Sunday morning and say that the church is full of hypocrites.

All sincere Christians are painfully aware of the imperfections of this earthen vessel that we call the church. It is imperfect because it is made up of imperfect people. So Christians prayerfully strive to make the church a more effective instrument for doing God's work on earth.

At the same time they see the glory of the church that many of its critics miss. To Christians the church becomes one of the greatest of all institutions because of the glory of the gospel it proclaims. Those who are blind to the beauty and power of the gospel cannot see the glory of the church that communicates it.

I. THE NECESSITY OF THE CHURCH

But is the church really necessary? If the gospel comes first, why not exalt it and let the church go?

1. Needed to Keep Alive the Gospel

The answer to that question is that the church alone keeps the gospel alive.

Once there was a man who wrote his friend, "I believe in Christianity. But I don't believe in the church."

His friend replied, "You cannot really believe in Christianity without believing in the church."

He was right. Why? Because without the church there would not be any Christianity in which to believe. The gospel has not come down to us by chance. It has been passed on through Christian groups of every generation who preached, taught, heard, and lived that gospel. They are the true apostolic succession. Without them, in their organized effort, the gospel would have died in the first century. The Bible too has been kept alive by the church.

We say that we believe in democracy, and we do. Can we believe in democracy unless we also support the institutions that keep democracy alive? Of course not. If we say we believe in education but do not believe in public and private schools or in colleges and universities, we do not really believe in education. If we say we believe in medicine but do not believe in medical schools, hospitals, and prescriptions, we do not believe in medicine. So it is with the gospel and the church.

We find in Christianity, then, two things: (1) the ageless gospel (good news) that has come to us through Jesus Christ and (2) the church that is its earthly instrument. Without the combination of these two things there would be no Christianity. The gospel of God in Jesus Christ is unutterably beautiful. It wonderfully answers our deepest needs because the gospel came from God just for that purpose. This gospel must be proclaimed and taught by a community of prayer and faith from one generation to another. When one Christian dies, another must fill the void. The community of prayer and faith moves onward.

The church maintains the gospel by holding fast to the Bible as God's living word that comes to finality in Jesus Christ. The church preserves and proclaims the gospel through its creeds, prayers, sermons, hymns, and deeds. (Speaking of our hymns, I regard *The United Methodist Hymnal*—which was approved by the General Conference in 1988—as the finest in all Christendom.)

Newborn babes start in spiritual nakedness. They need guardians who can wrap them in the garments of Christianity, so the gospel demands an organization that outlives the generations of believers. Christians come and go, but the fellowship of the redeemed continues through the centuries.

If the gospel is God's message, the church, despite its imperfections, is God's means of keeping that gospel alive.

2. Christian History Confirms This

We believe the church is necessary because of the facts of Christian history. The gospel has always been made effective by the church, which is the body of Christ (Romans 12:5; 1 Corinthians 12:27; Ephesians 4:12, 15-16).

Paul was a great man. Why? Because of the letters he wrote that make up a large part of the New Testament.

Why did he write those letters? He wrote most of them to strengthen the churches he had founded. Wherever Paul went, he disclosed a passion for founding churches. He took the ageless gospel of salvation in Jesus Christ and gave it a body in the form of the Christian churches at Galatia, at Philippi, at Thessalonica, at Corinth, and at Ephesus. He wrote to those Christian groups in order to encourage and counsel them. In this way Paul brought Christianity westward and was chiefly responsible for making it available to us in the Western world. Could the gospel have come our way without such churches? Of course not.

Once more, John Wesley was an extraordinary man. What did he do? He preached many sermons. Yet we are told that George Whitefield, who was a friend of his, was a better preacher than Wesley.

Who can compare the lasting influence of the two men, however? What was the difference? This. Wherever Wesley went, he was concerned to set up Methodist societies where New Testament Christianity could thrive. Whitefield was more content to preach and leave the rest to God. John Wesley had the passion and the genius for getting Christians together into a living fellowship of the redeemed. These Methodist societies eventually became the Methodist churches that are spread out all over the world. Without Wesley's mighty organizing work under God, Christianity everywhere would be immeasurably poorer.

The study of history shows that there is no sustained force without an institution. It reveals also that there can be no continuing Christian gospel without the church.

3. Our Human Situation Requires the Church

We believe the church is necessary because of the demands of life. This becomes as clear as noonday when we face the facts of our human situation as they really are.

We live in a world where evils are not limited to wicked individuals. The forces of evil are organized. They would destroy the church if they could. We confront not merely this evil person or that. We confront syndicated powers and principalities of evil. Crime is a *social* force. Evil forces are organized. Even the demonic practices of men brutalizing their wives and children are often supported by the failure of our criminal justice system. The mass media—with their extensive organizations—often add to the forces of crime, infidelity, dishonesty, alcoholism, and sorry living.

How can the dangerous forces of our modern day be overcome? Not by pious individuals who separate themselves from one another. We can be sure that the days of many contemporary ideologies are numbered. We know that long after people are sick of the sound and fury of these movements, they will be marching under the banner of Christ. Christianity is composed of a community of believers who do not fight the forces of evil as isolated individuals.

We see the significance of the church as soon as we know that we confront organized evils. As Paul said, "For our struggle is not against enemies of blood and flesh, but against the rulers, against the authorities, against the cosmic powers of this present darkness, against the spiritual forces of evil in the heavenly places" (Ephesians 6:12).

Unorganized goodness is no more effective than any other kind of unorganized power.

Turning from these larger issues of our world to our inner

problems, we find that we easily forget God. We need the church to keep reminding us of the reality of the spiritual.

It may be theoretically possible for some individuals to continue in a vital Christian experience without the church if they have had a fine Christian background. Practically speaking, however, it does not work out that way. Take a live coal out of the fire, and it quickly loses its glow. Take people out of the fellowship of the redeemed, and they soon lose their faith.

We may summarize by quoting from the Confession of Faith of The United Methodist Church (Article V): "Under the discipline of the Holy Spirit the Church exists for the maintenance of worship, the edification of believers and the redemption of the world." The church is not an end in itself: it is God's instrument for carrying out God's holy purpose in this world.

II. THE GLORY OF THE CHURCH

The glory of the church is the ageless gospel it proclaims. What are the ingredients of that gospel that make it so welcome to us? They are the mighty affirmations of our religion. These, as they are embodied in Jesus Christ, give us hope. They are therefore the good news.

In this light let us stand off and behold the glory of the church in its divinely appointed mission. By the church we United Methodists do not mean just our own fellowship. We mean all those churches that rightly bear the name of Jesus Christ.

1. The Message About God

Behold the glory of the church that from age to age persists in reminding us that God is in charge of this universe! We are not, like so many corks, bobbing up and down on an alien sea, for God is with us. God is the first and final act. We are not alone.

2. The Message About Jesus Christ

Behold the glory of the church that from generation to generation persists in reminding us that the best that ever walked the earth was Jesus Christ! In a world whose standards are often cheap, where success is measured in the coins of this life, where tyrants stalk about, where people are trampled underfoot, what is it worth to hear one voice exalting Jesus Christ as Teacher, Savior, and Lord?

3. The Message About the Savior

Behold the glory of the church that proclaims the great redemptive work of God in Jesus Christ so that everyone can enter into the Kingdom! People seek their messiahs in many places. They go and do not arrive; they seek and do not find. Then they meet the Savior through the church. What is it worth to have one voice that persists in reminding us from century to century of the forgiveness of sins? We sin and do not know where to turn. We hear the gospel and know that where sin increases, grace abounds all the more (Romans 5:20). Then we take the broken fragments of what we call our life to the foot of the cross and there receive the Savior's healing word and power.

4. The Message About the Dignity of Each Person

Behold the glory of the church that reminds us from age to age of the dignity and value of each person under God! Others speak of the rights of human beings and of their dignity. We travel with them as far as they are able to go. Only the church can put the full dimension of depth into this emphasis. Why? Because only the church sees people in the light of the God who created them and who cared enough to suffer and to give himself for their redemption.

5. The Message About Vocations

Behold the glory of the church in its call to see every useful task as a divine vocation! No job is merely a pay check. It is a task to be done for the glory of God and the service of ourselves and others. No work is a sacrifice. It is a privilege. For God calls us to it. What is it worth to have one voice teaching us never to be triflingly employed but to do our work with all diligence because that is pleasing to God?

6. The Message About Missions

Behold the glory of the church that, in the midst of our provincial perspectives, calls us to the world mission of Christianity. Because we need the Savior, all people need him. The church challenges us with the ideal of world fellowship in the family of God. It makes this challenge concrete by sending its sons and daughters to the far-flung corners of the earth with the message of the love of God. These missionaries carry no guns, earn no wealth, gain no high position; but, armed with the love of Christ, they heal the sick, teach the ignorant, train the unskilled, and proclaim the good news. As a body they compose the finest group of men and women who have ever walked this earth.

7. The Message About Responsible Living in Community

Behold the glory of the church that, amid a world of indifference, dehumanization, and desperate need, calls on Christians to do a great work for the betterment of people in society. The church, as the bearer of the good news in Christ, is called of God "to proclaim release to the captives," "to let the oppressed go free" (Luke 4:18), and to promote peace. For all its failures and weaknesses, the community of prayer and faith is still summoned to join hands in realizing the prayer:

> Your kingdom come.
> Your will be done,
>   on earth as it is in heaven.

8. The Message About Eternal Life

Behold the glory of the church that keeps reminding us that we are made for two worlds and not just one! We are made for the life everlasting. It begins here, but it does not stop at the grave. The greatest single miscalculation that can be made by the human mind is to suppose that death is the end. What is it worth to have one voice telling us that Easter is not just a day on the calendar? It is a fact about human destiny. Easter is God's perfect way of promising us personal immortality through Jesus Christ. For, according to the New Testament, it is not enough merely to say that we contribute to the everlasting life of God only to be sluffed off into oblivion. Because Christ lives, we too shall live.

III. SUMMARY STATEMENT

The church is the body of Christ. It is his instrument. It is his servant. It is the bearer of the eternal treasure, the gospel. Because Christ is the foundation of the church, "the gates of Hades will not prevail against it" (Matthew 16:18).

CHAPTER 13

We Believe in the Kingdom of God

THE BIBLE IS A BOOK about the kingdom of God. From beginning to end it speaks of the God who is vitally concerned with human affairs in this life. Some would confine the work of God to the personal needs of individuals. This is not the total insight of the Bible.

As we have already seen, we United Methodists believe in personal salvation. God loves individuals and redeems them one by one. We know that our Lord's earthly ministry was frequently to needy individuals. So we hold fast to the perfect relevance of the gospel to our profoundest personal needs. Yet Christianity can never stop there. Why? Because God does not stop there.

How do we know this? We know it from the Bible. We know it from Christian history. We know it from Christian experience and insight. We know it from the Christian vision of human needs.

I. THE BIBLE AND THE KINGDOM

One of the most basic ideas running through the Bible is that of the kingdom of God. We cannot get away from it.

1. The Old Testament Speaks

The Old Testament deals not only with individuals but also with the people of Israel. God's promise to Abraham concerned his descendants. It had much to do with the larger affairs of this earthly life. (See Genesis 12:2-3, 7; 13:14-17.) So it was with Jacob. (See Genesis 28:13-15.) The entire story of the great Moses reveals God's momentous yearning for the well-being of the enslaved people of Israel. The Ten Commandments concern the ordering of an earthly society under God. The writings of the psalmists and the prophets show God's holy purpose for the entire social order.

2. The New Testament Speaks

So it is with the New Testament. When we first see the Master as he enters on his divine mission, we hear him say, "The kingdom of God has come near" (Mark 1:15). This Kingdom was confined neither to the hearts of individuals nor to the world to come.

Jesus wanted to save the souls of individuals, but he also wanted to change the life of the Jewish community. He came to give abundant life to multitudes. In the light of what Jesus taught and how he lived, it is infinitely pathetic to tear his message loose from the total fabric of our human situation. He said he was sent to "proclaim the good news of the kingdom of God" (Luke 4:43). The whole story of his teachings can best be summarized in terms of this Kingdom.

Jesus made every effort to change the religious and social situation of the Jewish community. So far as Jesus was concerned, God's work was not being done as it should be through the religious leaders at Jerusalem. Even the Temple was polluted. When he cleansed it, he challenged the existing order at a point where it needed it.

In contrast to our human traditions and standards, Jesus came to announce the divine order. When he defied the regulations about the sabbath, he tore into the social fabric of the Jewish community. No regulations were more pervasively social than those concerning sabbath observance. None were more jealously guarded.

Yet Jesus called for an entirely different conception of the sabbath. He insisted on the life-subserving purpose of all regulations when he said, "The sabbath was made for humankind, and not humankind for the sabbath" (Mark 2:27). No saying could have placed him more decisively in the center of the social setting of his day. One of the basic reasons why the religious leaders stirred up the unthinking mob to shout, "Crucify him!" was that Jesus proclaimed the neglected social principle that the law of Moses existed for all. Those passages in Matthew 5 that read: "You have heard that it was said to those of ancient times ... but I say to you"—those passages tell the story (Matthew 5:21-48).

Jesus did not come into the world to call people merely to a life of personal and private serenity. He wanted them to have all the peace of soul that was possible. Above all, he wanted them to know their place and mission in the divine community.

II. THE DIVINE ORDERS AND THE KINGDOM

The God of the Bible is concerned with communities in the here and now as well as with individuals. God stood in judgment over Israel and over the nations. If the Bible is true, is it not obvious that at many points God is at war with our society? For God's will is being flouted by the sins of people in their interpersonal relationships. We scoff at God by waving our little standards in God's face. We say, "What difference do our racial prejudices make to God? What difference does it make if we blunder into war? What difference does divorce make to God? Why worry about dishonesty in business and corruption in politics? Does God care?

God has put us together in a community life. God has established certain orders on this earth. God wants God's purpose for these divine orders to be carried out. But what are the divine orders? They are the conditions that God has established for all civilized existence. Let us look at them.

1. The Economic Order

First, there is the economic order. God has put us on this earth to be trustees of everything in it. (See Genesis 1:26.) We are to get our food and shelter from it. We are to have comforts and conveniences because of our control over nature. All this requires the economic order, so God has established the conditions of farming and business and labor.

We waste the materials of the earth and pollute this beautiful little planet. We thus mock God. We ruthlessly exploit our fellows and thus trample on God's ordinances within which we are supposed to carry out our trusteeship. At no point in the economic order are we more defiant of God's will than in our ways of handling waste, and particularly, hazardous waste.

In the economic life we need always to let "reason and the will of God prevail." What does this mean? Basically it means absolute honesty and justice in all transactions. It means serving God with wealth. It means putting in an honest day's work.

At this point we United Methodists join all Christians in affirming the sacredness of all useful work. It is a joy to work. Every needed task has its glory in the kingdom of God. Every craftsman and artist, every doctor and lawyer and nurse, every teacher and home builder and preacher, every scholar, scientist, and writer, every business person and laborer, every political leader and journalist, everyone having to do with television and radio, every social worker, every servant of those who are differently abled—every young person and adult is called to do his or her work for the kingdom-building purpose of God.

2. The Political Order

Then there is the political order. No community life is possible without government. So the order of government was established by God. God is concerned about the quality of the governments of this earth. There is a vast difference in the eyes of God between democracy and tyranny. God's kingdom is defied by tyrants at one extreme and by indifferent citizens at the other. God's kingdom in the political order is repudiated by corrupt politicians and by officials whose soul can be bought for a price. Government exists for the glory of God and the service of people.

We Christians cannot be isolationists. We cannot separate ourselves from what happens in the governments of the earth. Why? Because God has established the order of government, and people have often corrupted that order. Not infrequently the fate of humanity hangs on these political organizations.

We United Methodists believe in active participation in government. Many Methodists participate in the affairs of national and local governments. Our prayer is that they will be true to their heritage. We believe that all Christians have a God-appointed kingdom-building job to do in the interest of good government.

3. Marriage and the Family Order

Again, there is the order of marriage and family life. This too has been established by God. Here also God is often defied by people. Our task as Christians is to become kingdom-builders by entering into the joys of creating Christian homes.

What kind of home is a Christian home? First of all, it is one in which God reigns. We belong to God and so do our family relationships. Second, a Christian home is one in which the husband-wife relationship is more important than any others. This is not to minimize in the least the wonderful attachments of parents and children to one another. But in a Christian home the husband-wife relationship comes first. This is not a human injunction; it is a divinely established order. Jesus said: "From the beginning of creation, 'God made them male and female.' 'For this reason a man shall leave his father and mother and be joined to his wife, and the two shall become one flesh.' So they are no longer two, but one flesh. Therefore what God has joined together, let no one separate" (Mark 10:6-9; see also Ephesians 5:31).

Husband and wife are bound to each other by the intimacies of a common memory. As life goes on, they rejoice together. Each one so contributes to the other that one is in a true sense lost without the other. God has made it that way. Every attempt to break this relationship—with rare and justifiable exceptions—is an attempt to defy the order that God has established for our earthly communities.

A wedding is an event, but a marriage is an achievement.

In the third place, a Christian home is one in which the children are loved and guided and taught every day. We are to love our children. We are to teach them the precepts of God. We are to show them by word and deed the light of the gospel. Every child must learn about God and Christ and love and fairness. Clearly the major responsibility here belongs to the parents.

In single-parent families, God's work is done by this same devotion to God's will and purpose. Every mother or father can be sure of God's unfailing grace. This grace of God is seen also in the help that comes from fellow Christians who are called to do what they can to nurture families in Christian formation.

4. The Educational Order

In addition to these divinely established orders, there are certain institutions without which no highly civilized life would be possible. These too are instruments of God for advancing the Kingdom.

To mention one in particular, there is the educational order. This includes our preschools, elementary and high schools, and colleges and universities. It is true that life could, in a manner, continue without these institutions. Since no advanced community life would be possible without them, however, we are justified in speaking of this educational order as having its ultimate origin and sanction also in God. Every Christian is called on to advance the Kingdom by devotedly serving and helping to finance our schools and colleges and universities. We United Methodists have demonstrated our belief in education by laboring to build educational institutions of high quality.

The work of the teacher is exalted because it follows in the line of the great Teacher and renders an indispensable service to humankind. The work of the student too is important. Every student, from preschool to graduate school, is called of God to do his or her best.

III. THE KEY PRINCIPLE

Within all these orders, foremost in our thinking must be the passion to know and do God's will. We find the key to that will in the love of Jesus Christ. In the light of that love we clearly recognize the diseases that plague the societies of this earth.

If God is in Christ, war has no place in the kingdom of God and must be conquered in the name of the Prince of Peace.

If God is in Christ, political corruption, indulgence in alcoholic drink, drug addiction, vulgarity, gambling, and pornography are enemies of Christ and must be overcome by Christian integrity and purity.

If God is in Christ, poverty and ignorance have no part in the kingdom of God and must be banished from the realm.

If God is in Christ, racial prejudice does not belong in human societies and must be cast out by the mighty power of the love and wisdom of Christ.

If God is in Christ, disloyalty and strife in the home have no place in the Kingdom and must be replaced by loyalty and understanding.

If God is in Christ, the wonderful gift of sexuality is not to be cheapened but to be exalted and expressed—in full respect for ourselves and others—in the divine rule: in singleness, chastity; in marriage, fidelity.

If God is in Christ, lawlessness and violent protest are not the ways to do a great work for God and our fellow human beings.

If God is in Christ, wrong laws and cumbersome legal processes need to be transformed for the service of all.

It has often been remarked by sociologists and other astute observers of society that no community will be able to maintain the highest moral standards and values unless it sees them as rooted in God. Many would join Pitirim A. Sorokin, a well-known sociologist, in saying that the best way to avoid calamity in the world was expressed by Jesus when he said, "Strive first for the kingdom of God and his righteousness, and all these things will be given to you as well" (Matthew 6:33).

CHAPTER 14

We Believe in the Life Everlasting

OURS IS THE religion of the empty tomb and the risen Christ. We United Methodists join all Christians in affirming the resurrection of Jesus and the life everlasting.

I. THE NEW TESTAMENT WITNESS

None of the writers of the New Testament doubts the resurrection of Jesus for a moment. None of them fails to grasp its towering significance in the Christian religion.

The Gospel writers all tell the story of the empty tomb. All of them speak of the risen Lord. Three of the Gospels (Matthew, Luke, and John) present detailed accounts of the appearances of this risen Lord. It is beyond all question that without this absolute affirmation of the Resurrection the Christian movement would have been reduced to a band of trembling moralists whose enthusiasm would have run out before their death.

The disciples were crushed by the Crucifixion. With what interest and excitement and doubts they listened to the first reports of the empty tomb! With what eagerness two of them ran to the tomb to see for themselves! With what overpowering joy they beheld their risen Lord!

Here was one of those turning points in history. Everything was changed. The past was gone. The cross was a triumph. The grave was defeated. The way was now open for the Holy Spirit to do its wonderwork on Pentecost.

On receiving power from on high, Peter stood before a multitude already sympathetic with Jesus and proclaimed the crucified and risen Lord. (See Acts 2:23-24.) Afterward some

116

three thousand souls were added to the fellowship of believers. (See Acts 2:41.)

Nobody grasped the significance of the Resurrection more firmly than Paul. He said, "If Christ has not been raised, then our proclamation has been in vain and your faith has been in vain" (1 Corinthians 15:14; see Romans 8:34).

To the first-century Christians, then, the Resurrection of Jesus was significant, not only because it established beyond all question that people could not destroy the Savior and his work but also because in the Resurrection there was the promise of everlasting life to everyone who lives by faith in the Son of God.

In the light of the New Testament, then, the efforts in recent decades to reduce the resurrection of Jesus to the faith of the earliest Christians are misguided. They are often supported by great learning and profound scholarly sincerity. Yet they fail to explain the impact of the risen Lord on the creation and sustenance of the Christian communities. The New Testament makes it clear that without the Resurrection, there would have been no continuing Christian movement. The reality of the church is explained, in part, by the fact of the Resurrection and the promise of our continued existence as individual souls after death.

II. OUR PROFOUNDEST QUESTION AND GOD'S ANSWER

When we turn from the New Testament to our own souls, once again we see how perfectly this teaching answers our most urgent questions. In the innermost recesses of everyone is the passion to live. This passion to live beyond the grave is nothing but an extension of the desire to live tomorrow.

In our modern setting we may ask this profoundest of all questions: What is the meaning of our earthly careers in the face of death? No question can probe deeper than this one. One who has no answer to death has no answer for life.

Why do we persist in asking about life and death and destiny? The answer is that we cannot help it. No passion goes deeper than the passion to live. No answer is more desperately sought by us than the answer to the question: After death, what? This is the cry of the soul for an enduring meaning.

God heard this age-old cry and called on Jesus Christ to reveal God's concern for us all. In the Savior, whom God raised from the dead, God revealed the holy purpose to overcome death. What we could never conquer, God conquered in Jesus Christ. It is precisely this marvelous adjustment of the gospel to our deepest needs that assures us that it is of God. We cry out like infants in the night, and God comes with the magnificent response.

III. WHAT IS ETERNAL LIFE?

What is this eternal life that is ours through Christ?

First of all, it is a life that begins here. Whenever the risen Savior reigns in our hearts, we become new creatures and start on the journey into everlasting life.

Second, eternal life means that each one of us, as an individual, will live beyond death. In other words, we believe in individual or personal immortality. It is not merely a matter of the "immortality of influence," about which so many speak. It is far more than the thought that in some way we shall contribute to God's eternal being while our souls are snuffed out at death. For what is most important is our souls in their continuing person-to-person relationships with God and others.

In the third place, eternal life is not merely endless existence. Mere existence has no special value. Eternal life means the opportunity for endless creative adventure with God. We cannot now imagine the vast projects that God has in mind. We know, however, that with God we shall not be content merely to sit around and rock our way through the centuries. God does not call us to laziness here; God will not call us to unemployment in the world to come.

Finally, eternal life, which begins here and contains even now the promise of unbelievably greater things, is a life of peace and joy. Why? Because it is lived in intimate association with God and with those who love and serve God.

Eternal life is one of peace and joy also because it is free from the sufferings, obstacles, and bewilderments of this earthly life. In it there is both a great work to do and the God-given power to complete it. Creative work is always a joy. It is a privilege even on earth to be asked to do any worthy job. This privilege will become transfigured in heaven.

Besides this, eternal life is one of peace and joy because it brings together the redeemed souls into a perfect fellowship. Many people ask, "Will we recognize our friends in heaven?" The answer is that we shall not only recognize them; we shall see how truly wonderful they are. We shall more perfectly love them.

Others ask, "Will we be married in heaven?" Jesus answered this clearly when he said, "In the resurrection they neither marry nor are given in marriage, but are like angels in heaven" (Matthew 22:30). This leads those who have known the joys of married love on earth to feel that heaven will lack something. We need to think more deeply here. Instead of the usual attachments of marriage, such as those we know on this earth, there will be spiritual attachments of the most perfect sort. Those who were bound to each other by a genuine love in this life will also be bound intimately to each other in heaven. Their relationship will be unspeakably more wonderful than the happiest marriages on earth could ever be. They will know each other. They will have a special relationship to each other. They will adore and serve each other. They will glorify God together in perfect worship and praise and service.

Moreover, all those to whom we were deeply attached here will be among our dear ones in heaven if we do not deny our Lord. Beyond this the whole society of the redeemed will be a community of love and joy. The only exception to this will be when the redeemed in heaven are called on to suffer vicariously with the brokenhearted Father of us all over the pathetic plight of those who have defied the aims of God. For we must never forget that God suffers even while reigning in heaven.

IV. SOME QUESTIONS ANSWERED

Many people have difficulty believing these things.

Some ask, "Why isn't the immortality of influence enough?"

The answer is that influence is not the most important thing. Not all the influences of history are to be compared to the value of the souls of people.

Why is any influence important? Because it helps people. If the people are so unimportant as to come to absolutely nothing at death, what difference does the influence really make in the end? Even a small child should not be deceived by the effort to put the immortality of influence—which is not immortality at all—in the place of a genuine life after death. Moreover, as we have already noted, the theory that we have everlasting life only because we contribute to God's everlasting being is contrary to the New Testament teaching on personal immortality.

Others say, "All this is merely wishful thinking. People believe it because they *want* to believe it. How do we know it is true?"

The desire to live beyond death is no different, in quality, from the desire to live tomorrow. Yet these people question the former and praise the latter. Of course we wish to live beyond death. We do not believe that our wish can bring it to pass, however. We believe in the Resurrection and the life everlasting because God has promised it in Jesus Christ. What God has promised God has the absolute power to perform. It is not and cannot be our doing.

Still others say, "But death is so final. It seems to be the end of everything. Our souls are so bound up with our bodies that it is hard to see how they can live on after the bodies pass away. After their death we never seem to communicate with people. How can these things be explained?"

The soul is one thing and the body is another. In this life the two are so intimately bound up with each other that our physicians are right in treating body and soul as one and the same thing. In fact the two are distinct. Thoughts, purposes, values, memories, have their entire existence in and for living souls. Just as the light is not the same as the light bulb, so a soul is not the same as the body that convoys it through this life. We Christians believe that at death we lose these corruptible bodies and at the resurrection are given incorruptible bodies that are suitable to the new dimension of existence beyond death. (See 1 Corinthians 15:42-44, 53-54.)

If souls live on, why do we not communicate with them after they have departed? Many people claim that they do. There are not a few reports on the subject. We must remember, however, that the dead are now in a different realm of existence. In the nature of the case, communication with the dead is not so reliably evident as it is among those of us who still live together in the same earthly dimension. A great gulf separates us from one another.

The question may still be asked, "How can these things be?"

Truth is stranger than fiction. There is no greater mystery than the birth of a baby. At every birth an entirely new creature enters into existence. How? We know the successive stages. Yet we have no insight whatever into how a human being who did not exist can now come into the world. This is a mystery of God's creative power. Yet it is a fact.

Many a person who accepts the miracle of birth without batting an eye stands completely baffled before the miracle of resurrection. We are familiar with the daily miracle of birth; we are not familiar with the miracle of resurrection. Our familiarity or unfamiliarity with these things has nothing to do with the realities. For ultimately everything depends on the power and purpose of God. In the resurrection of Jesus, God demonstrated the conquest of death and the policy of conquering death.

One question remains. Some say, "But does not this belief in the life everlasting incapacitate us for living effectively in the here and now?"

It has often been supposed that this belief shuts the door to a sensible interest in the practical affairs of this earthly life. In some cases this has happened. As a generality, however, persons who shirk their duties here are not the ones who have a lively hope for the everlasting life. Why? Because in the Christian affirmation this life and the next are vitally linked to each other. How we live here has a great deal to do with what happens to us in the world to come. So the fact is that, far from making us lose our sense of duty here, the assurance of eternal life becomes one of our finest springs of action in this life.

Our commission is sure. Our duties stretch out before us. During the only life we now possess, we are to work and serve humanity and advance the Kingdom.

V. THE DIVINE JUDGMENT

Christians have always recognized the terrible contrast between heaven and hell. It is our belief that we cannot express ourselves more clearly about our duties before God than by saying this: *How we live here makes all the difference between heaven and hell in the world to come.* We are not redeemed by our good works. We shall never be redeemed without them. Saved souls must do their duty before God and others.

Wesley insisted on this in the strongest terms. He never gave up the doctrine that we are saved by grace only. Yet he held fast to the affirmation that no one can continue to be saved without doing God's will on this earth. As Jesus said, "Not everyone who says to me, 'Lord, Lord,' will enter the kingdom of heaven, but only the one who does the will of my Father in heaven" (Matthew 7:21).

We have our God-given responsibilities in this world. We are called to carry forward God's work, in everything we do, as long as we live here. Then, and only then, can we hope to hear those words that are perhaps the most beautiful that anyone can hear, "Come, you that are blessed by my Father, inherit the kingdom prepared for you from the foundation of the world" (Matthew 25:34).

We believe in the life everlasting.

CHAPTER 15

Some United Methodist Perspectives

I. THE SECOND COMING OF CHRIST

WE UNITED METHODISTS know that the New Testament speaks in many places of the second coming of Christ. We hold that these references have a true meaning. While none of our Articles of Religion is devoted primarily to this doctrine, it is clearly mentioned in the Third Article. We affirm it when we recite the Apostles' Creed.

As a generality, United Methodists have so fixed their attention on the things of Christ that pertain to life here and now that they have not in practice gone deeply into the full import of the Second Coming. This is in part due to John Wesley's own commonsense way of viewing the matter. He believed the doctrine. Yet he always balanced his interpretation of it with practical good sense. By its very nature United Methodism avoids extremes here.

In regard to times and seasons, we keep returning to two statements by Jesus. He said, "But about that day or hour no one knows, neither the angels in heaven, nor the Son, but only the Father" (Mark 13:32). By implication this means that no one knows the century or the millennium. Again, the risen Lord instructed his disciples in these matters when he said, "It is not for you to know the times or periods that the Father has set by his own authority" (Acts 1:7). These words of our blessed Lord are, with us, final.

There is, however, a meaning in the Second Coming that we United Methodists do not want people to miss. This is the profound truth that God will bring this present order to an end in a way that is in keeping with his mighty act of creation. We cannot be true to the Creator and suppose that he would inaugurate a marvelous universe, create us for the realization of

123

a great purpose, be revealed in Christ, flow into our souls by the power of the Holy Spirit, only to let everything fizzle out in the end. Clearly the Christian understanding of the last things must be commensurate with our understanding of the vast processes of creation and redemption.

The Second Coming means then that, while no one knows the times or seasons, God will, in God's own time and way, inaugurate the new era under Christ in glory, power, and love.

As for our personal response to this, we have in our hearts the assurance of salvation, so we know that our life is in God's hands. At death, which may come at any time, we know we are prepared to take the Savior's hand and to walk in heavenly places. We believe that the Lord will meet us at the end of the line. (See John 14:3.) So we live in hope, regarding both our life after death and the new era that God will inaugurate.

The great point in Christianity, however, is not to wait eagerly for some event that lies hidden in God. The great point is to let the living Christ do his wonderwork in us now. As long as we are here on earth, we must be about our Lord's business.

II. THE UNPARDONABLE SIN

Some people make a great deal of the unpardonable sin. Yet it has never been viewed as a major doctrine during the long history of Christianity.

Why then all the talk about it? This doctrine goes back to a remark that Jesus made. When some Pharisees said that Jesus was casting out demons by the power of Satan (see Matthew 12:24), our Lord gave a strong answer. Among other things he said, "Therefore I tell you, people will be forgiven for every sin and blasphemy but blasphemy against the Spirit will not be forgiven. Whoever speaks a word against the Son of Man will be forgiven, but whoever speaks against the Holy Spirit will not be forgiven, either in this age or in the age to come" (Matthew 12:31-32).

We United Methodists believe that the only unpardonable sin is that for which people do not or cannot repent. When people, such as certain of the Pharisees, were so stubborn that they defiantly called God's work the devil's, they became hopeless. Jesus was talking about people whose pride was so great, whose blindness was so complete, that there was no basis for hope in them.

We United Methodists also believe that this thought can be overworked. We deplore the activities of those who frighten people into supposing that they might have committed the unpardonable sin. Here is where we need to look at the total insight of the Bible. We must never make light of God's mighty redemptive power in Jesus Christ by putting people beyond its reach.

For practical purposes we would give everyone this word of assurance: *If you fear that you may have committed the unpardonable sin, you can be sure that you have not done it.* Those who are involved in such sin never care enough to worry about it.

III. "WHAT IS TO BE WILL BE"

Some people say, "What is to be will be." So they leave everything to God.

We United Methodists do not accept this doctrine. We believe that everything happens under the rule of God. But we also believe that God created people with the power to say yes and the power to say no. From beginning to end the Bible calls men and women to "choose," to "come," to "repent," to "seek."

God created us with freedom. The facts of history prove beyond reasonable doubt that God does not interfere with that freedom. For this reason God allows people to go so far as to kill one another in war and destroy themselves on the highways.

We repudiate the doctrine of "what is to be will be." For it is a form of fatalism. It makes us helpless to do anything under our own God-given power. For this reason we put no confidence in astrology or predictions that imply fatalism or any other beliefs and practices that reduce human beings to puppets.

IV. "ONCE IN GRACE ALWAYS IN GRACE"

Other people say, "Once in grace always in grace."

What does this mean? It means that, after we have become real

Christians, we cannot fall away from the life of grace. In other words, it means that after we are Christians we have no freedom to turn away from Christ.

We United Methodists believe that we are still free to turn away from Christ even while we are Christians. Here again we take our human freedom seriously. Why do we think this way? Because both the Bible and common sense require it.

The Bible is filled with examples of people who started out well and ended up tragically. There was King Saul in the Old Testament. (See 1 Samuel 10:9-10, 16-24; 13:1-15.) There was Demas in the New Testament. (See 2 Timothy 4:10.) Besides these, many others might be mentioned. We can experience no state of grace that is beyond the possibility of falling. Human freedom functions at all levels of grace.

Backsliding is something that United Methodists preach and all denominations practice. Yet it is true that once we have tasted of the Christian life, we are not likely to turn away from it permanently.

V. PREDESTINATION

What is predestination? It is the doctrine that God alone decides who will be saved and who will be lost. It means that some people are picked out by God for salvation.

We United Methodists repudiate this doctrine. We affirm the sovereignty of God. We hold that only God can save us. We believe, however, that people may or may not put themselves in a position where God will do that saving work. God freely gives, but we must receive. We are saved by the grace of God only. To receive that grace we must confess our sins and trust in God's pardoning grace in Jesus Christ.

More than this, we United Methodists regard it as both contrary to the total insight of the Bible and to common sense to suppose that God would fore-ordain that anyone go to hell. Taken in its literal form, this is a pernicious doctrine.

We believe in a Christianity that is open to everyone. We call everyone to choose God and live.

VI. BAPTISM AND INFANT BAPTISM

We believe in infant baptism. Along with nearly all Christians we believe in baptizing older people whenever the occasion requires it. We are quite willing to immerse people if they so desire it. Since we hold that the amount of water used is not important, however, we commend the practice of baptism by sprinkling.

Originally infants were baptized because it was believed that their human nature was so tarnished by original sin that if they were to die they would be lost forever. If we turn this thought around and look at it from God's side, we come to the heart of the matter. All through the ages, Christians have believed that infants are unutterably precious to God. God does not want them to be lost. Infant baptism, however, goes deeper than any supposed cleansing from the pollution of original sin.

To see the point of infant baptism, we need to understand the sacrament of baptism. Whether for infants, children, or adults, all baptism has the same meaning. It is the sacrament of incorporation into the community of faith. In baptism, we become members of the church; we become heirs of the long history of God's acts of salvation; we are born again by water and the Spirit. In and through baptism, the Spirit works in the life of the believer and the life of the church to bring to reality the benefits of the new era.

Why do we United Methodists join the vast majority of Christians in recognizing the importance of infant baptism? Because by birth God marks and seals little children and claims them for God's people. Because God's mighty redemptive work in Jesus Christ has already been done in behalf of each infant, and the church celebrates that fact. Because the whole community of faith, along with the family, needs to lift up each little child and claim him or her for Christ and his church in advance of the age of accountability. In all things, including religion, the infant goes with the family.

Baptism is an act of the Spirit through the community of faith. In infant baptism the community does for the child what, with prayer and proper guidance, the child will do when confirmed and brought into the membership of the church. Baptism gives the true meaning to confirmation. For, in the case of infants, confirmation is a mere delay in time of the organically unified process of incorporation into the community of faith that began at baptism.

Another way of putting it is that the Holy Spirit works mysteriously through the community of Christ to claim each infant for God and the Kingdom.

Against this background we United Methodists deplore certain errors in thought and practice pertaining to infant baptism. For one thing, we deplore the error of thinking of baptism as a ceremony for the benefit of the parents. It does or should give them an increased sense of responsibility before God for the Christian nurture of their child. The sacrament goes far beyond that, however.

Again, we deplore thinking of infant baptism as a mere ceremony of christening. It is true that at baptism the child is given a Christian name by the church. Yet infant baptism is real baptism, and therefore does not require being repeated.

Once more, we deplore the spoiling of this great sacrament by the use of a flower dipped into the water and placed on the infant's head. Why? Because that has no historic significance. No flower can take the place of the hand of the minister of God placed directly on the infant's head. We are dealing here with a profound spiritual mystery, not a touching ceremony.

VII. THE LORD'S SUPPER AND OPEN COMMUNION

United Methodists have not always appreciated the importance of the sacrament of the Lord's Supper. In this we have often failed to recognize our identity as a historic community of faith in the line of Christ and the apostles. Jesus himself inaugurated this sacrament and commanded his followers to observe it.

This sacrament awakens a holy memory of what Jesus Christ has done for us and for the whole world. It fixes our minds on the fact of our sin and on our need for forgiveness. It communicates God's love for each soul. Mysteriously, through the bread and the cup, the Holy Spirit moves in our midst to bring home to us, both personally and in community, the effects of the great work of Christ in our behalf. Therefore, this sacrament is a celebration of God's redeeming love and empowering grace. It means our grateful acceptance of God's gift of forgiveness and new life. It means renewed commitment and resolve.

We deplore those efforts at innovation that cheapen the deeper meaning of this sacrament by types of music and liturgy that do not authentically communicate what Jesus Christ has done for us. We welcome experimentation here, but the innovations should not tamper with the theological substance. The elements need to be chosen with the historical connection with Christ's passion and death in mind.

One of the enduring values of this sacrament is its unalterable focus on Jesus Christ and him crucified as a central verity of the Christian religion. Sermons may or may not do this. The music may or may not do this. Small groups in the church may or may not do it. In this sacrament God's action in Christ is the central reality.

We deplore also the practice among Christians of excluding fellow Christians from the Lord's Supper, for we believe in open Communion. In some groups Christians sit down together and talk of church union, but they cannot kneel together before the Lord's Table. What a mockery! This is deplorable on all counts— historical, theological, ecumenical, and experiential. Not even a relative from another denomination can enter into this service, not even a friend, not even a ministerial colleague in the fight for liberty and justice. Few facts on the contemporary scene illustrate more tragically the breakdown both of intelligence and of good faith.

Let all who sincerely repent and are in love with their fellows, or who long to be, come to the Table of the Lord!

VIII. PRAYER AND INTERCESSORY PRAYER

We believe in prayer.

Prayer is not merely asking God for things. Nor is it merely "saying prayers." It is more than meditation. It goes deeper than contemplating. Prayer has been called "the soul's sincere desire." It is that and much more. Some identify prayer with action. This too misses the mark.

What is prayer? It is person-to-person communion and encounter with God. It involves some real awareness of the greatness, glory, mystery, and love of God. In important respects, prayer differs from our person-to-person fellowship with other people. It is communion with God, the Creator, Sustainer, Redeemer, and Empowerer of our lives. God shares himself and his benefits with us. To be sure, God delights in the responses of the children of God and is enriched by them. We are the ones, however, who receive God's blessings and benefits in prayer.

Jesus was the only founder of a world religion to teach his followers to pray to God as Father. This is of first importance in the kind of prayer we have been talking about. If prayer is person-to-person communion with God, it helps us to pray when we think of God as like a loving parent. This means that while God has priority as Creator and Sustainer, God is infinitely approachable. God is to be thought of as the ultimate Person. This does not mean that God has a body as we do or that God is limited as we are.

Rather, it means that the basic characteristics of a person—as distinguished from a stone, a tree, or a galaxy—apply to God. God *knows* us. Without this, there could be no person-to-person communion. God *loves* us. Without this, we would avoid God. God *communicates* with us. Without this, prayer would be reduced to talking to ourselves. God acts purposively. Without this, prayer would lead to aimlessness. God *summons* us. Without this, we would not be empowered to serve the present age.

Broadly speaking, there are two kinds of prayer—prophetic and mystical. In the former the person-to-person communion with God, involving the call to serve, is primal. In mystical prayer—which is represented not only in the religions of the East but also by some Christians—there is the ascent leading toward the vision of God or the sense of complete oneness with God. Both of these have their places. The biblical revelation, however, guides us basically into the kind of prophetic prayer discussed in the foregoing paragraphs. As Heiler points out in his great book entitled *Prayer*, the highest point in the history of prayer was reached when Jesus prayed in Gethsemane: "Yet not my will but yours be done" (Luke 22:42).

The greatest answer to prayer is a life dedicated to the service of God and others.

We believe also in intercessory prayer.

This means that we believe in praying for others. Some people imagine that the only kind of prayer that does any good is the kind that works on our own minds. We United Methodists go much further than that.

Jesus prayed for others. (See Luke 22:31-32; John 17:9-17.) By example, Jesus taught his disciples to pray for each other. Paul and others followed this practice with great persistence. (See 2 Corinthians 13:7-9; Ephesians 1:15-17; Philippians 1:3-5; 1 Thessalonians 1:2-3; Philemon 4.)

What happens in intercessory prayer? Many things. Put it like this. Suppose that every time we prayed for someone else, God put a thought, a reminder, a suggestion, into the soul of the other person. Then God would be answering our prayer. This would not mean that the other person had to do what we wanted. It would mean that when we prayed in the right spirit, God would always answer our prayer. Such prayers often perform wonders.

Nor do we rule out divine healing. We United Methodists deplore some of the practices along this line. We support and foster the medical profession with its scientific understanding and proven skills. Also we know that many people have been healed as a result of prayer. We see no conflict between these two approaches. Here we are frank to say, however, that we do not understand the laws of divine healing, so we refuse to let people deceive themselves with vain hopes. In any case, intercessory prayer, as well as the prayer of the patients, is an aid and support to the work of the doctors. It is a mighty healing force.

Besides this, intercessory prayer is one of God's ways of binding the hearts of people together and doing God's great work in the world.

We believe also in praying for the church and for world peace and for the kingdom of God.

IX. WHY DO PEOPLE SUFFER?

Many people believe that all human suffering is caused by sin. We United Methodists repudiate that doctrine. We know that much suffering comes from sin. Generation after generation suffers from the sins of the parents. Greed and stupidity bring war. Disloyalty brings broken homes. Drunkenness brings disaster. Corruption in high places brings disgrace. People sow what they reap. (See Galatians 6:7.) "The way of the faithless is their ruin" (Proverbs 13:15).

The way of innocent people is sometimes hard too. Why? We do not know. Turn it around any way you like, and you are baffled in just the same way that the innocent Job was.

I once heard a well-known preacher say, "If a loved one gets cancer, it is because God sent it." We United Methodists repudiate that as not only inhuman but as utterly contrary to the revelation of God in Jesus Christ.

Jesus did not come into the world to show us the God of terror. He came to show us the God who heals our hurt. Jesus was the Great Physician. We cannot use God to explain innocent suffering and at the same time look to him for help in rising above it.

We know that innocent people suffer. We know also that they are not alone in their suffering. It is a lonely business, but frequently God comes nearest to the children of God in the time of their suffering. There is no night so dark but that God's light shines through. With God's help, which is ever present, we can be not merely conquerors but "more than conquerors" (Romans 8:37).

God seems to permit such natural evils as hurricanes, tornadoes, cancer, deformity, insanity, and so forth, for some reason that we do not now understand. Yet we know God loves us still and would never deliberately harm innocent people.

X. THE WORLD MISSION OF CHRISTIANITY

We believe in world Christianity.

Why? Because we need the gospel; everyone needs it. John Wesley caught the true spirit of that earliest missionary commission (see Matthew 28:19-20) when he said, "I look upon all the world as my parish."

We must adventure or decay. Life is like riding a bicycle: either we go forward or get off. A Christianity that loses its evangelical dynamic is itself lost. Through churches, schools, hospitals, farms, industries, and all serviceable agencies, we believe in preaching and teaching the unsearchable riches of God in Jesus Christ around the world.

Only Christ can answer the deepest questions of life. Sin? Forgiveness. Fear? Faith. Despair? Hope. Resentment? Love. Provincialism? World vision. Death? Everlasting life.

We believe in the unity of all people in Christ. We believe that, through well-qualified missionaries and through well-trained leaders from their native lands, we must labor together to communicate the love of Christ. This means a sharing in the prayers for the world. It means giving time and money to do a work for God so great that it reaches around the whole world.

XI. THE ECUMENICAL SPIRIT

We United Methodists are proud of our heritage. We believe that the best contribution we can make to the ecumenical movement is to bring to it a profound appreciation and growing understanding of our own identity. At the same time, we earnestly desire to work cooperatively and creatively toward greater unity in spirit, organization, and leadership among all Christians. Wesley insisted on the "catholic spirit." His sermon on that topic contains some of the finest remarks on tolerance in all Christian literature. The ecumenical spirit may begin with tolerance—in the full meaning of that word—but it goes beyond it to seek agreement and unity wherever possible.

To that end it has been often suggested that United Methodism is *catholic, protestant,* and *evangelical.* It is catholic (universal) because it shares in the biblical revelation and in the vast, rich, cumulative tradition of Christianity. It is catholic in its call to all United Methodists to share in the efforts toward Christian unity.

United Methodism is protestant in that it takes the Bible seriously. It is protestant in calling its people to share in the responsibility for soul-searching and critical re-evaluation. It is protestant in that it respects the conscience of every person and calls on all to seek, to perceive, to understand for themselves. It is protestant in protesting against everything that is phony and demonic in the church and in the lives of "religious" people.

United Methodism is evangelical in its emphasis on a living relationship with God through Christ. It is evangelical in that it seeks to win the world for the Kingdom. It is evangelical in striving toward this end by the conversion and rededication of individuals and by the transformation of society. It is evangelical in calling on all United Methodists in their own ways to grow in their effectiveness as living witnesses of what God has done in them and of what God can do through them.

The ecumenical movement began with the Edinburgh Conference in 1910. During the period since then many advances have been made toward Christian unity. There is a long way to go, and we may never make the journey all the way. But conversations are taking place. We are getting better acquainted with each other. Proposals—sometimes wise, sometimes impractical—are being made.

I think particularly of the Catholic-Methodist dialogues that were initiated, on our side, by the World Methodist Council in 1966 and, on the Catholic side, by the Secretariat for Promoting Christian Unity. From year to year these conversations have continued. The major differences—some of which are fundamental—have been identified. The vast areas of agreement have also come to light. For example, our agreement with the Roman Catholics in diagnosing the problems and diseases of the modern world is notable. In the realm of spirituality we share not only in a common heritage since the days of the apostles but also in the emphasis on the aim toward sanctity or holiness. On both sides the stress on sanctity has its individual and social dimensions. We are agreed that the spiritual life in community must manifest itself in justice, peace, goodwill, and constructive leadership.

This is only one small dimension of the ecumenical quest. There are others too numerous to mention. This much is sure. Wherever Christians are concerned to meet and share, to work together in the struggles against inhumanity and mediocrity, to worship together, to pray together, and where practicable, to organize into a common fellowship—there we United Methodists are present and at work.

XII. THE MINISTRY AND THE LAITY

We United Methodists believe that all Christians, by virtue of their baptism and their Christian experience, are called of God to serve in the world where they are. We believe in the priesthood of all believers. Every person has as direct access to God as any other. The overwhelming majority of Christians are laypersons— men and women, children and young people. In a true sense they are all ministers or servants of God.

So it was in the earliest days of Christianity. The multitudes who followed Jesus, the individuals who sought him and to whom he ministered, the women who stood by him to the end—these were laypersons. The stories Jesus told were, for the most part, about laypersons. The good Samaritan, the widow, the shepherd seeking a lost sheep, the father and the prodigal son, the sower, the faithful steward, the searcher for the pearl of great price, the builder, the householders, the workers in the vineyard, the rich fool, the woman and her lost coin, the rich man and Lazarus, the judge, the tax collector—these were all laypersons. One reason why laypersons have been so responsive to the Master is precisely because he rubbed shoulders with them and talked their language.

The story of the laity has never been adequately told. We United Methodists, however, try to give due recognition to the judgment and leadership of the laity by requiring that there be a layperson for every minister at the major deliberations of the church. In the local churches the leadership of the laity, of dedicated men and women, children and young people, as always, is of utmost importance.

As every layperson knows, the ordained ministry is essential also for the leadership and direction of the church. It was no accident that Jesus selected twelve to devote themselves wholly to understanding, preaching, and witnessing to the good news. (See Mark 10:28; Acts 1:23-26.) The ordained ministry goes back to the apostles. While all are called to serve God, some are called to devote their whole mind, heart, and soul to understanding and interpreting Christian truth, to guiding the spiritual life of the community of prayer and faith, and to leading in all moral and spiritual affairs. Therefore, this is a special call of God. It is sacred. Vast oceans roll between those who think of the ordained ministry as a profession and those who experience it as a divine call.

We United Methodists believe the call to the ministry is of utmost importance. It may come gradually or suddenly. It may be experienced in any one of many ways. It may even be intermingled with doubts that come and go. It consists essentially of two things. First is the inner sense that God wants a person to devote full time to proclaiming the gospel and to leading in the spiritual life. This part of the call is usually nurtured in the home, in the local church, in Christian camps, and in the struggles and yearnings of the soul.

Second, the call requires authorization by the church. In United Methodism this authorization begins in the local church where a person has membership and continues through the district conference and thence, through the board of ordained ministry, to the annual conference. It is not enough for an individual merely to feel called. This, together with the appropriate response to God, is a part of it. One must demonstrate the determination and aptitudes for the demanding work of the minister in the contemporary world. The called person must prove willingness to serve by disciplined living, by pursuing an appropriate education, and by working under the direction of a bishop and district superintendent.

In The United Methodist Church there are two ways of giving full authorization to a minister; namely, by ordination and by full membership in an annual conference. Therefore our ministers are ordained at the annual conference to signify the mysterious ties that bind them to their conference brothers and sisters. For they share with them, work with them, are responsible to them. If United Methodist ministers fail to do their work with creativity and skill, they let their congregations down, they let themselves down, and they let their conference colleagues down. Most of all they let their Lord down. So United Methodist ministers have a great honor and a heavy responsibility placed on them.

Ministers thus called are not to regard themselves as spineless, unthinking, passive servants of the church. They are called for creative leadership. With God's help, they are chosen for that resourceful, courageous, and patient leadership under Christ that these times of mediocrity and tragedy require. They may discover new and better ways of doing things, but the essential content of their message is the same.

The ordained ministers are nurtured and encouraged by Christian laypersons. Congregations and other arenas of servant ministry rejoice that these persons come as Christ's gifts. They hold fast to the view that whoever is appointed deserves their prayers and full cooperation. For the ministers represent not themselves but Jesus Christ. In love they remind the people that God's ways are not their ways and God's thoughts are not their thoughts. They seek to woo the people to God and to encourage them to grow in Christian character and to improve their Christian witness and service.

We United Methodists join all Christians in recognizing that the advancement of the work of Christ in the world depends entirely on the eagerness of the laity and the ordained ministers to join their minds and hearts in doing a great work in the world with God's help. For together we pray and labor to change the lives of people by spreading scriptural holiness over the world!

STUDY
GUIDE

John O. Gooch

SESSION ONE

Getting Into the Study

Introduction and Chapter 1

1. Welcome the group members. Ask them to introduce themselves by answering three questions:
   Who am I?
   How am I?
   What do I bring to this session?

For example, a person might say, "I am Kay Allen. I have a bit of a sinus problem tonight, but I'm basically fine. What I bring tonight is a curiosity about United Methodism, since I was raised in another denomination."

2. Tell the group that this study is a quick look at United Methodist beliefs and how they help us live in the world. It is about what is distinctive in United Methodism and why we consider that distinctiveness important. Remind them that it is a "quick look." When you finish the study, there will still be questions and the need for learning more. Such is the basic reality of life: the more we learn, the more we learn we need to learn.

3. Point out the core doctrines and emphases given in the section "A Common Heritage: Beliefs and Practices" (pages 9–16 of the book). Tell the group that you will be dealing with the Bible in session two, salvation in sessions four and six, Christian habits and disciplines in session three, and holiness in sessions six and seven. For this session, we will take a closer look at how United Methodism is Arminian in our understanding of our relationship with God.

Tell the group that Wesley lived in a time when the dominant theology was Calvinism, built on the work of John Calvin in Geneva, Switzerland, and John Knox in Scotland. We are familiar with Calvinism because the Puritans, Presbyterians, and Baptists are all Calvinist in their background and theology. Wesley's theological position was in conscious opposition to Calvinism.

Put on a chalkboard or large piece of paper the following outline of Calvinism, and tell how Wesley opposed each point. Calvinism can be summarized in the word *tulip:*

Total Depravity. (Humanity is totally sinful and cut off from God.) To this, Wesley put the idea of prevenient grace, which says God is always working in our lives and we are not cut off from God.

Unconditional election. (God does everything necessary for salvation; there is nothing we can do.) Wesley said that God, indeed, saves us (justifying grace) but that God also calls us to work together toward salvation. Our faith and good works in response to God are part of salvation (what we call "cooperating grace.")

Limited atonement. (Christ died only for those who are predestined for salvation.) Wesley said that God's will is for all to be saved. Only our refusal to accept God's gift prevents our salvation.

Irresistible grace. (If we are among the elect, we will be saved whether we want to be or not.) Wesley put a strong emphasis on free will, insisting that we are free to accept God's salvation or to deny it.

Perseverance of the saints. (Sometimes called "once in grace, always in grace.") Wesley was convinced that even the "perfect Christian" sins and that we are in continual need of renewed forgiveness and grace. "Backsliding" is an important Wesleyan doctrine.

Ask for questions for clarification. Remind the group that the point is how God and humans work together in salvation. Have the group members read the fifth and sixth paragraphs in the section "Arminian in Our Relationships With God" (page 13). Check to be sure everyone is clear on the distinction between predestination and saving ourselves. Tell them that the Wesleyan position is in the middle. God and humans work together in salvation.

4. Remind the group that the final core emphasis is being called to share what we have experienced. Ask them to read the third paragraph of the section "The Call to Share What We Have Experienced" (page 15) to find the three elements in the message we are called to share.

5. Note that United Methodism is both vital and balanced.

Ask the group members to name the four elements Bishop Stokes lists in the section "United Methodism Is Vital Christianity" (pages 19–21). These are all referred to as "more than." Remind the group that "more than" rests on a foundation of "at least this much. . . . "

Then ask the group members to name the five "balanced views." (See the section "United Methodism Is Balanced Christianity" [pages 21–25].) Form five small groups and ask each group to look at one of the five balanced views. (If you have fewer than ten people, one person may need to be a group.) Each group should be prepared to report to the total group on what that United Methodist view is and what makes it "balanced." Encourage them to report in their own words and not just to read the text.

6. Assign Chapter 2, "We Believe in the Bible," as the reading for the next session. If all read the material before they come to the session, they will be able to dig deeper into the issues.

7. Close the session with a prayer of thanksgiving for the group, for the church, and for John Wesley and our other ancestors in the faith. Ask for guidance and blessing for persons as they read and study during the coming week.

SESSION TWO
The Bible
Chapter 2

1. Begin the session by reading this statement: "We believe the Holy Bible, Old and New Testaments, reveals the Word of God so far as it is necessary for our salvation. It is to be received through the Holy Spirit as the true rule and guide for faith and practice" [Articles of Religion, Article IV, *The Book of Discipline of The United Methodist Church,* page 65]. (You may want to write this statement on a chalkboard or large piece of paper before the session.)

Ask the following questions: What does that statement not say about the Bible? (For example, it does not say that the Bible is without mistakes, that it is the ultimate Word of God, or that it is a law for our lives.)
What does the statement mean when it says "the Word of God so far as it is necessary for our salvation"?
What does the "true rule and guide for faith and practice" mean? How strict is the rule and guide?
Is there room for us to interpret and apply the Bible to new situations and understandings, or are we locked into the literal words?

Note disagreements (if any) among the group members, and point out that one of the great strengths of United Methodism is our diversity. We may not agree on everything about the Bible, for example. In fact, we probably will not. But we can agree that the Bible contains the truth necessary for salvation. Also note any questions that cannot be dealt with in this session, either because they are too involved or because you do not feel qualified to deal with them. Suggest ways persons can find the answers.

2. Look at some things the Bible says about itself. Ask half the group members to read 2 Timothy 3:16-17 and the other half to read John 5:39-46. Ask each small group to report on what they

find: What does this passage say about Scripture? Remind them that, in historical context, these writers were talking about what we call the Old Testament when they said Scripture. The New Testament had not been written and canonized yet.

Then ask: When you look at the two passages of Scripture side by side, how do they compare?
Do they say the same thing?
Do they seem to be contradictory?
Which one feels more comfortable to you?
What is each passage saying about how we use the Bible?

3. Point out that Bishop Stokes says the Bible is "ageless." Ask: What are some ways he says the Bible is ageless?
How are those ways true for us?

4. Then ask: What are some ways the Bible has been particularly helpful and meaningful for you?

5. Assign Chapters 3, 4, and 5 for reading before the next session.

6. Close with a prayer of thanksgiving for the Bible and for wisdom to understand it and apply it to our lives.

SESSION THREE
The Triune God
Chapters 3, 4, and 5

1. Begin by asking: Why do you believe in God?
How do you intellectually justify your belief? (Record answers on a chalkboard or large piece of paper.)

Then ask for a quick review of why Bishop Stokes says we believe in God (pages 34–39). Are there major differences in the two sets of reasons?

2. Take a look at some biblical ideas about God. Assign each of the following passages to an individual or small group. Ask them to read the passage and be ready to describe to the total group in a few words what the passage says God is like.

Job 1; Isaiah 40:1-23; Ezekiel 34:11-31; Job 38; Isaiah 43:1-13; Hosea 11:1-9; Amos 2:6-16

As individuals report, list their responses on a chalkboard or large piece of paper. Ask: When we look at the list, what do we see?

Are there differences/disagreements among the images? Remind the group that God is greater than the sum of all the ways we try to describe God.

3. Make a brief comment on the Trinity. Stress two points. First, there is a language problem when we talk about the Trinity. The Trinity is not God, Jesus, and the Holy Spirit. The correct way to describe the Trinity is to say God is Father; God is Son; God is Holy Spirit. Second, the Trinity is a mystery. We can think of many analogies to describe the relationships among the three persons, but ultimately they all fail. As Philip Watson was fond of saying, "It's best not to inquire too closely into the home life of the Deity." That is, we can never understand the Trinity because God is so much greater than we.

4. Remind the group of the old saying, "If you want to see what God is like, look at Jesus." Ask: Based on what you know about Jesus, what is God like?

What does Bishop Stokes say we know about God from looking at Jesus? (See Chapter 4, "We Believe in Jesus Christ," pages 45–49.)

Read or tell the story of Jesus and the disciples at Caesarea Philippi (Mark 8:27-30). After Jesus asked what the disciples were hearing, he asked them the most important question they would ever face: "But who do you say that I am?" That is also the most important question we will ever face: "Who do you say Jesus is?"

5. Look at what Bishop Stokes calls the primary sources for an understanding of the Holy Spirit. (See "The Holy Spirit in the New Testament," pages 50–53.) Assign one of the following texts to each person or small group. Ask them to read the text carefully and to be prepared to report on what it says about the Holy Spirit.

John 14:15-17; John 14:25-26; John 15:26-27;
John 16:7-11; John 16:12-15; Acts 2:1-13;
1 Corinthians 12:1-3

As persons report, list their responses on a chalkboard or large piece of paper. Ask: Does what we have here hold together?

If this is an accurate description of the Holy Spirit, then what works might the Spirit be doing in our lives? in our church?

What ought we to expect the Spirit to be doing? Call attention to what Bishop Stokes suggests about the work of the Spirit in the sections "The Language of the Holy Spirit" and "The Fruit of the Spirit," (pages 54–58).

6. Summarize what you have talked about in the session.

Ask: What issues about the Trinity do we need to continue to work on in the future?

What are some ways we could do that?

7. Assign Chapters 6, 7, and 8 for reading before the next session.

8. Close with a prayer of thanks for the work of God in your lives and your church. Ask for guidance for this week and for the future.

SESSION FOUR
A Hunger for God
Chapters 6, 7, and 8

1. Begin by saying: One of the great intellectual puzzles of our time is, "What makes humanity unique?" We used to answer "language," or "tool-making," or something similar. But we now know that other animals make tools; other animals communicate with one another. We cannot even answer "love," because several species mate for life and mourn when they lose their companion. The Scripture suggests, as does Bishop Stokes, that humans are unique because we are "created in the image of God."

Ask: What do you think that means?
Is it a physical image?
If so, which one of us looks like God?
Or is it something else? What do you think?

2. Read aloud Psalm 8:3-8. Ask: What does this psalm say about humanity?
How does that exalted language square with the reality of today's headlines?
Is the human creature who is perpetrating all this evil really that close to God?
Just what does it mean to be human?

3. Look at some other biblical images that suggest ways in which Jesus saw people. Read each of the following stories aloud, and then ask: What did Jesus see in this person?
Why did Jesus respond to this person the way he did?

Mark 10:17-21, the rich man
Luke 23:39-43, the repentant thief on the cross
Mark 7:24-30, the Syrophoenician woman

What can we learn from Jesus about how to look at other people?

4. Ask: What are the "six divine redemptive facts" Bishop Stokes puts forward about the cross? (See the section "The Meaning of the Cross," pages 69–71.)

Form six small groups. Ask each group to report on one of these facts. They should plan to describe the fact briefly and then tell why it is important. The reports can include examples and questions.
When all have reported, ask: What do we believe about the cross? What questions or problems do we have about the cross?

5. Look at some headlines. Either have copies of several issues of the newspaper with you, or report on the top stories you have heard on the news.

OR

Ask the group: What did you hear on the news today?
What's going on in the world?

Then ask: What do the headlines suggest about the reality of sin in our lives? Obviously, the news had some stories about personal sins.
Did you also catch anything about collective sins?
What was there about racism, sexism, and so on?

With the headlines in mind, turn to the Bible. Matthew 5:21-48 is the part of the Sermon on the Mount in which Jesus talks about the power of sin being deeper than surface acts. This long passage is broken into sections, each with its own subhead, in the New Revised Standard Version of the Bible. Ask individuals or small groups to read each of the sections.

Then ask: Why do you think Jesus is going deeper than the conventional morality of his (or our) day?
What does that suggest about sin?
Given who said all these things, if we take them even halfway seriously, how can we not say we are sinners?

6. Look at the answer to sin: God's grace. If you can, have the group sing one or two verses of "Amazing Grace." If singing is not a good idea, at least read the first stanza aloud together. Remind the group that this hymn was written by a man who had been active in the slave trade but who gave that up when he became a Christian. God changed his life completely.

Define *grace* as "God's love actively seeking us."

7. Explain the idea of justification, which Bishop Stokes talks about in the section "Justification by Faith" (pages 75–76). *Justification* is a legal term that means being set right with the law. Paul used it to say we are set right with God. It is as if we were on trial before God because of our sins. Clearly, we are guilty. But, just as sentence is passed, the judge (God) leaves the bench and comes to stand in our place to take our sentence. We are "justified," treated "just if I'd" never sinned.

8. Assign Chapters 9 and 10 for reading before the next session.

9. Close with a prayer of thanksgiving for God's grace and salvation and hope for our future in God's hands.

SESSION FIVE
Living a Christian Life
Chapters 9 and 10

1. Tell the group about John Wesley's pattern of disciplined living. He rose at 4 A.M., prayed for an hour, studied for an hour, ate breakfast, then went about a day that was carefully planned. He resolved early in his life to spend time praying, studying the Bible, observing the Lord's Supper, and doing good works. He rode over 25,000 miles on horseback preaching; wrote dozens of sermons; published hundreds of books; administered schools,

clinics, employment agencies, and credit unions; appointed the preachers; ran the conference; and had time left over to beg money for the poor. Wesley was able to do all that, and more, by the grace of God.

Remind the group that the reality is, we cannot accomplish any goal, no matter what it is, unless we discipline ourselves to work toward it. Ask: What are some goals we have (or have had) in life that we can reach only through constant discipline and effort? (Making the team, playing a musical instrument, writing a book, and finishing school are all examples that come to mind.)

2. Bishop Stokes reminds us of some promises for living the Christian life in the section "The Bible's Promise" (pages 79–80).

Ask: How do you react to those promises?
Do you think they might be true?
Call attention particularly to what Bishop Stokes says about "Ask–search–knock." Ask: What does that suggest about how we ought to deal with God's promises? (Here's a hint: God's promises are so extravagant that we may even be afraid to test them, just in case they turn out to be true.)

3. Ask: What does Bishop Stokes say are obstacles to victorious living? (See the sections "A Major Obstacle to Victorious Living" and "Another Obstacle to Victorious Living," pages 80 and 82.)
How are those obstacles real in your experience or in the experience of people you observe?

What does Bishop Stokes say are the "answers" to those obstacles? (See the sections "The Answer" and "The Answer," pages 81 and 83.)
Do they sound like realistic answers for life?
Why or why not?

4. Remind the group that, for Christians, love is the ultimate resource for life's struggles.

Form three small groups. Assign to one group the section "Jesus' Emphasis on Love" (page 85); to a second group, "Paul Speaks of Love" (page 86); and to the third, "What Is Love?" (page 87). Ask each group to present a summary report of what its section says, including digging deeper into the Scriptures listed there, if they would like.

5. Ask the same three groups to reflect and report on the sections "Love in Today's World" (page 88); "Love in Solitary Souls" (page 88); and "Love Implies Both Law and Wisdom" (page 89).

6. Ask: What have we learned about living the Christian life?
Given the harsh realities in today's world, from armed guards in the schools to random murders and drug buys on the streets to wars and threats of wars all over the world, does saying "love is the answer" seem simplistic?
Why or why not?

7. Assign Chapters 11 and 12 for reading before the next session.

8. Close with a prayer that God will help us learn to love as God loves.

SESSION SIX
No Solitary Salvation
Chapters 11 and 12

1. Tell the group: We have talked about sin, about God's gift of love for us, about justification, and about living the Christian life. In this session we are going to talk about conversion, assurance, holiness, and the church. All of them are tied together.

2. Conversion is a gift of God, a being "born again."

Ask: What images come to your mind when you hear words like *conversion* and *born again*?

How do you feel about those words and images?

Is that language with which you are comfortable?

Why or why not?

How does Bishop Stokes define/explain conversion and new birth?

Is his explanation helpful for you?

Why or why not? (See the section "What Conversion Is and Why We Believe in It," pages 91–94.)

3. Ask: When we want to be assured of something, what is it we want?

What do we mean by assurance or reassurance?

Given the ways we have said we understand assurance or reassurance in our world, what do you think "assurance" might mean as a part of our relationship with God?

How does Bishop Stokes define *assurance*?

Why does he say we believe it? (See the section "Assurance," pages 94–95.)

4. What is "scriptural holiness"? This is a key United Methodist doctrine. Our original mission statement as a denomination included the phrase "to spread scriptural holiness over the land."

Ask: What, according to Bishop Stokes, are the six basic points about holiness on which all Christians ought to agree? (See the section "Scriptural Holiness," pages 95–100.)

Do we attain holiness by our own efforts in moral living, or does it come some other way?

If we took seriously the idea of holiness, or "going on to perfection," what kinds of changes would we need to make in our lives?

5. John Wesley said, "The New Testament knows no solitary religion." By that he meant that we cannot be the Christians God

calls us to be, or even the Christians we want to be, by ourselves. "Worshiping God on a creek bank" can be a meaningful experience; but as the only experience of worship we have, it is totally inadequate. We need the church. We cannot find new birth, assurance, or growth in holiness without the church.

Form three small groups, and assign each group one of the subpoints under "The Necessity of the Church" (pages 101–105). Each group should plan to present a report on what its section says, plus a "minority report" arguing that Bishop Stokes cannot be right. Ask each group to give an explanation. This exercise will provide a series of "mini-debates" with the book.

6. Ask: Can you remember some times in your life when the church was especially important to you? Perhaps a time when you were in real spiritual need and the church was there for you? Or all the faithful persons who taught you the faith and modeled the Christian life for you? When has the church been important? Would you be the same person without the church?

7. Assign Chapters 13 and 14 for reading before the next session.

8. Close with a prayer of thanksgiving for God working in our lives in and through the church.

SESSION SEVEN
Now and Forever
Chapters 13 and 14

1. Tell the group that the language of "kingdom" is sometimes seen in our day as oppressive. The cultural and political "tags" we hang on the idea of kingdom get in the way of understanding the Scriptures. In addition, the role of kings in the modern world is radically different from the role of a king in Jesus' day. God is not

a constitutional monarch, like Queen Elizabeth, who has the form of the office but very little power. In Jesus' day, a king was an absolute monarch, with total power over the lives of his subjects. So, when Jesus talked about the "kingdom of God," he was talking about God as absolute ruler over the church and the world.

2. With that caveat in mind, look at some biblical understandings of God's kingdom. Form three small groups. Assign one Old Testament and one New Testament passage to each small group. The group is to read the passages and be prepared to interpret for the group what the passages say about God's rule in the world.

> Exodus 20:1-17, The Ten Commandments
> Leviticus 19:1-18, A part of the holiness code
> Amos 5:10-13, 24, A mirror image of God's rule
> Matthew 13:44-46, The treasure and the pearl
> Matthew 22:1-14, The wedding banquet
> Matthew 25:31-40, The parable of the judgment

As groups report, list what they say on a chalkboard or large piece of paper. Then ask: If this is a fair picture of what God's kingdom is about, what should we be doing?

3. Tell the group that one way The United Methodist Church tries to live out God's kingdom is expressed in the "Social Principles," found in *The Book of Discipline*. The Social Principles are reviewed every four years by the General Conference and updated to fit the changing political, economic, and social situation. They are the only official voice of the church on these issues. If possible, show the group a copy of the Social Principles and point out the major categories or headings. In some ways, these parallel Bishop Stokes' subheads in "The Divine Orders and the Kingdom" (pages 111–14). Ask if there are topics on which anyone would like to know what the Social Principles say. Look up and read the relevant passage, if there is one.

Remind the group that the emphasis of the kingdom of God,

expressed in the teachings of the prophets, the life of Jesus, and the Social Principles, is on economic and social justice. Care for the poor, the weak, the marginalized, and the voiceless is the heart of the teaching of the Kingdom.

4. Tell the group that the Kingdom is incomplete in this world, but it finds its fullness in the life of the world to come. We believe in "the life everlasting," which begins with the resurrection of Christ. Look at 1 Corinthians 15:1-26, which has three parts:

(1) a list of the apostolic witnesses to the Resurrection (verses 1-8);
(2) an ironic playing with the idea that there is no resurrection (12-19);
(3) a discussion of the implications of the Resurrection (20-26).

(Note: To get the flavor of the idea that there is no resurrection [12-19], ask the group members to read each verse carefully, looking for the "if" and the "then." List these instances so that you get the full picture of this ironic argument for the Resurrection.)

5. Ask: What is eternal life? Bishop Stokes' description of eternal life has four parts. (See the section "What Is Eternal Life?" pages 118–19.)

What are they? Look at the parts individually. If each one is true, what does it mean for us?

6. Ask: What about the Judgment? This is an important question for many people who want to be sure that those with whom they disagree are going to be judged. What does Bishop Stokes say about the Judgment? (See "The Divine Judgment," page 121.) What do you think?

Remind the group of two points about judgment. First, Matthew 25 tells us we will be held accountable for our actions in this life. The basis of the accountability is not what we so often consider sinful but the question of social justice. What did we do about the poor and marginalized? Second, the ultimate judgment is in the hands of God. On the one hand, that's bad news. Who wants to have to be accountable to God, who is the only Person in the universe to whom we cannot say, "But you did. . . . "? On the other hand, that's good news. God is merciful, often more merciful than some of our brothers and sisters might be.

7. Assign Chapter 15 for reading before the next session.

8. Close with a prayer, asking God's guidance and help in living the life of the Kingdom.

SESSION EIGHT
Some United Methodist Perspectives
Chapter 15

1. Ask group members to decide which perspectives they would like to discuss. Have persons who are interested in the same question meet together. You may have several groups scattered around the room. Give each group the following questions:

(1) What have you heard about this topic?
(2) How does Bishop Stokes define it?
(3) What does Bishop Stokes say United Methodists believe about it?
(4) What questions or concerns do you still have about this topic? (Put these in writing.)

After fifteen minutes, form new small groups and repeat the process with different topics. In this exercise each person should be able to participate in a discussion of at least two topics about which he or she has some interest. If time allows, move to a third set of small groups.

158 / MAJOR UNITED METHODIST BELIEFS

2. Look at the lists of questions generated by the small groups. Suggest there is a lot of material there for future learning. Ask: As you take responsibility for yourself and your growth in faith and understanding, what do you want to do with these lists of questions? (For example, do you want to look for books to read on these topics? Are there short-term classes on some of these topics you would like for the church to offer? What comes next? What are you willing to do to help make something happen?)

3. Close with a prayer of thanksgiving for what has happened in the group and for the growth and joy you have experienced.